OVERWORKED

OVERWORKED

SUCCESSFULLY MANAGING STRESS IN THE WORKPLACE

DON HAWKINS

MOODY PRESS

CHICAGO

To the three children God has entrusted to Kathy & me:

Karen Joy Hawkins Justice
Donna Lynn Hawkins Hancock
Brent Edwards Hawkins.

You have each been a source of great joy,
and I thank God on every remembrance of each of you.

CONTENTS

THE STRESS TESTS

PREFACE

At almost five o'clock on a Friday afternoon, my computer flashed me the message "This will end your Windows session." My colleague Allen knocked on the door of my office. He and his wife, Jeanette (who had stopped by to pick him up), were headed out the door.

"How are you coming on your book about stress in the workplace?" Allen wasn't asking just from his inquisitive perspective as our chief staff researcher. During the preceding months he had provided me with a great deal of data for the book. In addition, he had survived fifteen years in one of the most stress-filled vocations of all, the pastoral ministry. From his own experiences as a pastor and from the people to whom he had ministered, he had learned firsthand just how stressful work can be.

"I hope to begin on the actual writing this weekend," I answered. "I have all the research in place. It's just, well, you know, with the stresses of the changes we're making in the broadcast and keeping up with the rest of the workload, I'm finding . . ." We both laughed heartily as we realized how stress in the workplace was making it difficult for me to write on stress in the workplace.

I suspect you may be able to relate to that Friday afternoon moment. Unfortunately, for many people stress in the workplace isn't a laughing matter. As we shall see in the following chapters, it's one of life's ugly realities, and it extracts a frightening toll physically, emotionally, and even spiritually.

Ever since God assigned Adam to care for the Garden of Eden, individuals have worked. Scripture makes clear that work is not simply a matter of drudgery but a part of the personal satisfaction and significance God wants us to feel. As we will see, stress can be good; indeed, without stress we couldn't survive. If we had no pressure of responsibility or deadlines at work, we probably would finish little. I recall one job I held during my college years. The workers were given almost zero supervision. Several of my fellow employees chose to do absolutely nothing with their work time, spending it reading, watching television, or playing games. Yet, ever since the Fall into sin, a person has had to earn a living "by the sweat of his brow." In other words, God predicted at the Fall that our work would be stressful. And such stress, in excess, can become harmful.

Many of us are living out the title of this book—we are truly overworked! Excess stress seems to have become much more of a fact of life today. I read one recent study showing that 71 percent of those questioned felt stressed out by their work, and 63 percent by financial pressures and problems. We will include much more statistical data in following chapters. Clearly, work creates stress.

Overworked will not merely recognize and discuss the problem. My personal passion in writing this book is to provide insight and encouragement from a distinctively biblical and Christian perspective. The goal is to help readers cope with the problems of excess stress in the workplace.

Our starting place, obviously, is insight. We need to get a handle on the problem, sense its magnitude, and discover how it impacts us. To help you gain such insight, most chapters will include a "Stress Test," a quiz or evaluation for determining your personal struggles with stress.

Part 1 will discuss the *extent* of stress in the workplace. If we are ever to experience freedom from the debilitating effects of overwork and workplace stress, we first need to understand the truth about it. Many centuries ago Jesus told a group of His followers, "You will know the truth, and the truth will set you free." Among the questions we will answer are:

How is my job stressing me out?
How does modern life contribute to my stress in the workplace?
What impact does stress have on my personal and family life?
What are the origins of both work and stress?

In Part 2 we will consider the *causes* of stress in the workplace. To what degree are the events and circumstances themselves stressing me out, and how much of my stress is due to perception? Almost eight years ago Frank Minirth, Paul Meier, Richard Flournoy, and I wrote *How to Beat Burnout*; we concluded that stress is one of burnout's three major causes. In fact, most people we talked with, when asked what causes burnout, almost automatically responded, "Why, stress, of course." However, in that book we warned that it's not quite that simple. There are other factors, such as having a driven personality and harboring bitterness. But stress is a major factor.

In *Overworked* we will examine the degree to which our perception of events and circumstances as stressful actually creates problems of stress. And since a big part of our stresses comes from what has been commonly referred to as "the tyranny of the urgent," we will look at priorities and urgent tasks to determine how they factor into stress. We will also examine the impact of various personality types and consider the "incompetency factor," often referred to as the Peter Principle, whereby individuals reach a job level that exceeds their skills. There they remain stuck in a very stressful and unsatisfying situation.

However, just looking at stress in the workplace and figuring out what causes it doesn't complete the picture. In the final section we will focus on *solutions* for workplace stress. Part 3 will begin with a "big picture" look at work and life's major priorities, which I have identified as a wholehearted commitment of love to God and unconditional love for people. We will also examine how work impacts us personally, especially in the area of motivation and attitude. Finally, any solutions to work-related stress must factor in ways to deal with people and resolve conflict. Since so much of our stress grows out of interacting with others, we will seek to discover and apply workable, biblically based strategies for conflict resolution, team building, and shared vision.

Many books have been written on the subject of stress, of course, and quite a few on work-related issues. But in reviewing recent books on these two subjects, I have found nothing that looks at stress and work in the same way as *Overworked*. From talking with individuals from all walks of life, I'm convinced that many of us need help in dealing with these work-related issues.

Of course, reading a book on a subject won't guarantee that you'll never have any problems with that topic. Early one Friday, as my friend Allen and I took our customary afternoon coffee break, he asked, "Don, how many books have you written on burnout?"

"Two—and I burned out both times."

The real issue isn't just understanding a subject like stress, overwork, or burnout. It's learning to apply the principles that can set us free from the negative effects.

In other words, the key to overcoming stress in the workplace—or any problem—is to recognize the truth of what Jesus told His disciples in the Upper Room. Interestingly, He made that declaration the night before He fulfilled the greatest work ever—dying on the cross to pay for the sins of all mankind. What He told them was, "If you know these things, happy are you if you do them." Jesus was saying that knowledge is important, but application of that knowledge is essential. I hope this book will go beyond knowledge to bring guidance and relief to your life as a worker and servant.

THE EXTENT OF STRESS
IN THE WORKPLACE

CHAPTER ONE

STRESSED-OUT
AND OVERWORKED

Several hundred government employees had just begun working in the high-rise office building by nine o'clock that Wednesday. A few had dropped their children off at the second-floor day-care center; they and their co-workers were now sitting at desks or moving along hallways toward their offices. They expected little more than another day of drudgery and minor crises.

Then, at 9:04 A.M. on April 19, 1995, a massive bomb exploded in front of the Alfred P. Murrah Federal Building in Oklahoma City. The blast tore away almost half the structure, leaving hundreds of Social Security workers, military officers, and other government workers either dead or seriously injured. Among the dead were more than a dozen of the children.

ULTIMATE STRESS

Though the savage destruction of the Oklahoma City explosion was an extreme case, it reminds us of the kinds of stress anyone can encounter in the workplace, and it adds yet another dimension to just how stressful going to work in the world of the '90s can be. Following the explosion, a *USA*

OVERWORKED

Today/CNN Gallup Poll of 601 adults revealed that 89 percent
thought a similar attack to be likely in the U.S. in the near
future. One out of five workers believed their workplace
could be a target, and nearly half of those surveyed, 46 percent, considered it impossible to prevent such attacks.[1] Like
a monster tornado ripping through the heartland, spinning off
damaging gusts from its super cell, the Oklahoma City explosion compounded the deadly effects of stress on the job.

The bombing of the Murrah Federal Building yielded a
rash of copycat bomb threats, which forced the evacuation of
many federal office buildings around the country. The Oklahoma City tragedy guaranteed stepped-up security measures
at government offices and corporate headquarters virtually
everywhere. Instead of open, free, and unfettered access to
workplaces, there would be metal detectors, surveillance cam-
eras, electronic access cards, employee IDs—even devices to
identify authorized employee access by fingerprint.

Though the bombing of public office buildings has added
another dimension to workplace stress, the responses in
Oklahoma City reflect the tensions many of us or our neighbors face in the workplace.

For instance, consider the stress of working with the public as a police officer, firefighter, nurse, doctor, or rescue
worker. In the Murrah Building, rescue workers crawled
through debris, discovering body parts and bloody clothing,
occasionally avoiding falling pieces of the building as they
tried to locate survivors. Nurses and doctors treated trauma-
tized, bloody victims, saving hundreds, yet losing others on
the operating table or pronouncing them dead on arrival.

Just hours after the incident, on my live call-in radio
program "Life Perspectives," I interviewed Russ, a Norman,
Oklahoma, fireman who also works part-time for a Christian
radio station in Oklahoma City. His voice breaking with emotion, he described some of the scenes at one of the Oklahoma City hospitals where victims had been brought. Then he
apologized. "I'm sorry. I'm supposed to be a professional fire-

fighter and a professional broadcaster, but it's just . . . overwhelming."

STRESS IN EVERY WORKPLACE

Stress in the workplace is far more widespread than one
exploding office building. It occurs in every workplace and
for a variety of reasons. Some time ago I sat in the coffee
shop of the Cornhusker Hotel in downtown Lincoln, Nebraska, sharing a booth with two fellow workers from our human
resources department at Back to the Bible, Tonya Fredstrom
and Linda Becher. The two women talked freely about stress
in the workplace and its symptoms. Tonya began by describing the symptoms of overworked, stressed-out employees.

Overworked employees have "emotions that are right on
the edge, fatigue, and absenteeism," she said. "We have one
employee who has been under a great deal of stress, who
hated to use up her vacation time but needed to take off to
deal with the stress she was feeling. Our department agreed
that emotional distress is the same as physical sickness, so
we let her use her sick leave. So she took a week off to try to
pull herself together."

Linda then mentioned a common fear that contributes to
tension in the workplace. "A lack of job security these days is
a huge factor in job stress. If people feel like they aren't performing very well at work . . . they think, 'Am I going to be
cut?' That probably causes performance itself to drop, and
the stress level rises."

Linda's comment reminded me of a family I knew. They
had purchased a home and a car based on the husband's
income in what looked to be a secure job. But a management
change forced him to leave his job for another position, cutting the family's income in half. As the man explained, "It
became an interesting scramble. We still have the house and
car, but it certainly added a great deal of stress."

"I think the overall economic situation adds to the gloom
of job stress," Linda said, bringing me back to our conversa-

tion. She recalled a scene in the Christian bookstore she had previously managed. "I remember people coming in buying copies of *The Coming Economic Earthquake* [by Larry Burkett] and they would say, 'How can we ever get everything paid off by the year 2000?' They'd come into the bookstore in Stress City because they're mortgaged to the hilt and there's no way they can pay all their debts off. They read these predictions and say, 'How am I going to survive?'"

"Those concerns even add pressure for me at age twenty-seven," Tonya added. "There's pressure to get financially organized. I look at my parents and see what they have in savings. My husband and I say we'd like to have this kind of security retirement plan, but what I have to remember is that I have to reach those goals over time. There definitely is a pressure to eliminate debt—pay off credit cards, not use credit cards."

Tonya's words about debt and credit reminded me about a "Life Perspectives" program on which Bettye Banks, vice president for Consumer Credit Counseling Service in Dallas, told about one family with "over thirty credit cards and one hundred thousand dollars in consumer debt—and that's not including house and car notes!" I'm convinced that many of our stresses at work are connected to pressures to survive financially.

WHAT IS STRESS?

At this point, let's stop and define the word *stress*. We start with a simple recognition: Stress is a fact of life. It goes with us to the office, follows us home, waits with us in traffic jams. A visit to the dentist, an upcoming exam, a boss's bad day, an approaching deadline, or company for dinner are all part of what we call stressful.

Stress is the combination of physical and emotional responses we feel as a result of unexpected major and minor events in our lives. Stress creates tension. In his landmark book *The Stress of Life*, Hans Selye describes stress as our

STRESS TEST

True or False?

Some time ago, while speaking at a corporate seminar sponsored by a large investment firm in Dallas, I gave a true-or-false test based on material included in my previous books *How to Beat Burnout, Before Burnout,* and *The Stress Factor.*[2] Why not take this test yourself and see how much you know about stress?

_____ 1. *Stress is caused by the events that happen to us.*

_____ 2. *We always know when we are under stress.*

_____ 3. *Stress affects only those with high pressure jobs or lives.*

_____ 4. *The only way to lower stress is to change your life or take medication.*

_____ 5. *Stress-free living is possible.*

_____ 6. *All stress is bad.*

_____ 7. *Emotions have a will of their own and cannot be controlled.*

Most who take the test are surprised to learn that every single one of these questions could be answered false! In the chapters that follow, we will learn why that is so.

....

body's response to any demand made on it—whether a good, positive kind of stress, an expected part of life that leads to happiness or fulfillment (what Seyle calls *eustress*), or *distress,* excessive levels of ongoing or damaging stress.[3] In other words, we might explain stress as the result of any event, major or minor, that happens to us.

The major events of life—the death of a spouse, a divorce, being fired, an income tax audit—obviously add significant pressure to our lives, and *pressure* is just another word for stress. In fact, the concept of stress actually comes from the field of physics, when outside force adds pressure to bend or distort another item. Think for a minute about all the forces that act on your life: a crying baby, an alarm clock, the washing machine overflowing, a flat tire, being stuck in rush-hour traffic, an argument with a spouse, a prodigal teenager, one more project added to an already heavy workload. Any of these things will add significant stress.

Now let's apply that definition of stress to the workplace. Stress occurs from those events, both major and minor, that take place during the job and that affect us both at the workplace and after hours, back at our homes. We have already looked at some of those events, including lack of job security. Others, seemingly less important, can become major contributors to stress, including the ringing of the telephone, the fax machine jamming, an overbearing boss, or a backstabbing fellow worker.

For many people what seems to be the fast track to success has actually become the superhighway to stress. Barry Zissmon, a fifty-five-year-old Dallas lawyer, talks about feeling constant pressure during his sixty-seven-hour workweek. He says his goal is "to be able to retire before I die."[4]

TYPES OF STRESS IN THE WORKPLACE

About a year ago, Kathy and I were invited to conduct a marriage retreat for officers from the Houston, Texas, police department. During that weekend, I had the opportunity to talk with Sam and Liz Nuchia. As Chief of Police in Houston, Sam underscored firsthand just how stressful law enforcement could be. "Don, my men and women are under incredible pressure. The work itself is hard enough, the hours often long. But the main thing is, every time they go to work they take their lives into their hands. Their spouses never know, when the doorbell or the phone rings, whether they'll be told something has happened. It's hard to even measure the negative effects of the stress of their work on their marriages and their families—not to mention their own physical health." That weekend I talked with numerous officers who told their stories of workplace stress: long hours, frustration, seemingly endless paperwork, even life-threatening situations.

Those are just some of the types of stress we face in the workplace. Maybe you have faced a few of them. Stories about stress from overwork can be told about almost any job, and the types of stress can vary. Consider these:

Jerry and Sam are creative marketers, considered among the best in the country and highly respected by their peers. Recently the company they worked for merged with another organization. Almost overnight they became answerable to a new boss who, as they put it, "doesn't understand the intricacies of our business and came in with new budget restrictions, workplace rules, and procedures that basically leave us working with one hand tied behind our backs." Both Jerry and Sam are feeling the stress of losing authority at work.

Dianna is an emergency room nurse in a major metropolitan medical center. Each shift is a "roller coaster of stress," as she puts it, with life-affecting decisions made on the run, sometimes without all the information needed. "It's like some of those television shows you see, only worse. The human suffering, the blood, the pain. Then there's getting chewed out by doctors, never having enough time to get everything done, not having the authority to do some of the things I know need to be done for my patients. I wonder why I keep doing it—but I love what I do. It's just the stresses that are killing me."

Mike once worked for a large electronics firm. Highly respected by fellow workers, he constantly found himself battling a boss who "felt threatened by how well I was able to do my job and the fact that, if I wanted to, I could have gotten him fired and taken his job. That wouldn't have been the Christian thing to do, but it certainly wasn't Christian the way he treated me."

Mike was finally told by his boss, after he had survived one round of corporate downsizing, "You'll be the first to go in the next round of cuts." Mike left his job and, with the aid of a small inheritance, started his own electronics and repair service business. "It was frightening for both me and my wife," Mike said. "I worked long hours, spent huge chunks of time putting together proposals that usually got turned down, mortgaged our family to the hilt, and found our marriage strained almost to the breaking point."

Betty is an executive secretary, competent and skilled, who found herself fired for allegedly not getting the job done after she exposed some illegal activities taking place in her company. "It was a real dilemma for me. My work was stressful but I enjoyed it, and I was good at it. When they asked me to look the other way about some of the things that were going on in the office, I just didn't feel like I could. So now I don't have any job stress—I just don't have a job!"

David, a high school teacher in "one of the roughest neighborhoods in town" finds stress from several sources, including kids who are verbally abusive and who sometimes strike out at their teachers, and parents who yell, scream, and otherwise try to intimidate. "Then there's the paperwork, the bureaucracy. Sometimes I think I spend three times as much time taking care of all that as I do teaching. Then there are those mindless hours of meetings."

George and Anna are food servers—George a waiter in an upscale restaurant, Anna a hostess in the coffee shop of a large hotel. Each must please a boss and customers with high expectations. Both enjoy their work, but both feel the effects of the stress. "I come home so tired, I feel like I've been running nonstop for hours," George says, "and sometimes it seems like, no matter what you do, it's not good enough. As a waiter I'm caught in the middle between customers who are unhappy and mistakes made in the kitchen."

Some jobs seem to entail special risks because of the working environment. As **a construction worker, Mark** puts

in long hours and faces backbreaking physical labor, exposure to the elements, and uncertainty about when he will be
called to his next project. His wife, Shelley, says, "We never
know from one day to the next how long the work will last or
when the next job will come along. Mark makes good money
when he's working. When he isn't, he draws unemployment,
as long as that lasts." From Mark's standpoint, the pressure to
meet construction deadlines, the risk of injury, and working
out in the elements—especially during long, cold Midwest
winters—are all hazards of his work.

An increasingly common cause of stress for many women
is sexual harassment. **Rhonda, an instructor at a university
in the South,** found it to be the major source of her job
stress. "I could keep up with the teaching load, the lesson
plans, grading papers, interacting with students—all of that.
But what I couldn't handle was a boss who was constantly
making comments that were out of line, putting his hands on
me inappropriately, and badgering me to go out with him. I
know they have procedures for dealing with this kind of
thing, but my boss was part of the 'good old boys club,' and it
didn't take me long to find out that complaining would just
cost me my job."

THE CHANGING WORKFORCE

On Labor Day 1993, the Families and Work Institute released a national study of the changing workforce—the first
of its kind since a 1977 U.S. Labor Department study—that
examined the work, lives, and attitudes of employees in companies ranging in size from Fortune 500 firms to the corner
drugstore.[5] Here were some of their findings:

80 percent said their jobs required them to work very hard.

65 percent said they must work very fast.

42 percent felt "used up" by the end of the workday.

At least one-third felt they did not have a "supportive
work culture."

Not only did those surveyed indicate their work to be stressful and difficult, they experienced a time gridlock, as the average workweek for full-time employees reached 44.3 hours. More than a quarter of those surveyed worked fifty hours, and 10 percent worked more than sixty hours per week.

More than 3,400 workers participated in this landmark study, and 42 percent of respondents worked for companies that had reduced their staff the previous year. So much for those previous predictions that advancing technology would allow companies to switch to a four-day workweek or shorter on-the-job hours!

According to Faith Wohl, the head of DuPont's work-and-family initiatives, "The workplace is becoming harsher, and there are higher expectations in terms of hours you put in and how hard you work."[6] She reports some managers asking people to work as many as sixty hours per week.

PLAYING THE SURVIVOR

Is the quality of work life a priority for American corporations today? "Not at all," says labor economist Audrey Freidman. He identifies the highest priorities as corporate cost-cutting and remaining competitive. In other words, although human resources departments have brought sensitivity to employees' needs at a certain level, the highly competitive modern environment of corporate mergers, business failures, and other marketplace factors has raised workplace stress rather than lowered it. Indeed, the Family and Work Institute survey indicated that 27 percent of those surveyed feel "emotionally drained from their work."[7]

Many employees have been forced to play the Survivor game. Between mid-1992 and mid-1993 almost half of 870 companies surveyed had downsized, two-thirds for the second year in a row.[8] David Noer of the Center for Creative Leadership in Greensboro, North Carolina, points out that those who survive the cuts also are not unaffected. "Survivor sickness is like the psychic numbing of post-traumatic stress disorder, the kind of thing suffered by soldiers after an intense battle, or rescue workers following a disaster like the Oklahoma City terrorist explosion. Fatigue, resentment, fear of future loss, even guilt over having survived the job cuts—it almost seems that many of the survivors suffer more stress-wise than those who have lost the jobs."[9]

The Survivor game is not fun, as those who stay on the job play the guessing game of "Who's next?" and "What duties do I have now that Jack is gone?" Sales and production quotas are up, and everything else, including operating budgets and expense accounts, are down. For managers, the corporate restructuring is "one of the most harrowing stress tests in business history," according to Donald Rosen of the Menninger Clinic.[10] Perhaps one of the most debilitating effects is that managers who were trained to build are now being paid to downsize and to fire. That's why work no longer energizes many individuals. Instead, it drains them.

RESPONDING TO STRESS

In order to put work-related stress into perspective, we need to understand how it affects us. Keep in mind that both major life events and minor life hassles contribute to our stress. The constant criticizing of a fellow employee or back-stabbing in the lunchroom can, over time, become as stressful as the threat of losing one's job. I'm convinced that the cumulative effect of minor stresses can sometimes seem greater than the stress of major life events. After all, we tend to prepare ourselves when there is serious illness, death, or other great difficulties, and often we have the support of others. But those inopportune flat tires, missing car keys, lost files, or forgotten appointments—though seemingly insignificant when taken alone—add up to a great deal of wear and tear on our lives.

How does stress—in the workplace and in the home—influence our physical responses? Primarily, adrenaline rushes into our bodies, charging our muscles and speeding our heartbeat, yet often giving us a heightened state of physical readiness with nowhere to go. One certified stress management instructor at Bryan Memorial Hospital in Lincoln, Nebraska, describes stress as a modern phenomenon brought on by the mismatch of today's environment and the body's "fight or flight" response, which centuries earlier was needed to cope with wild animals.[11] As a young man, the future King David of Israel worked at his first job as a shepherd. There he faced danger from wild animals—he even told about taking on a bear and a lion to protect his flock.

Instead of dealing with bears or lions, many of us today face irate customers, grouchy bosses, interrupting phone calls, broken equipment, or rush projects, but our bodies still respond as though they were facing a physical crisis; our blood pressure rises, muscle tension increases, and loads of adrenaline, fats, and sugars rush into the bloodstream for quick energy.

Some time ago while in Los Angeles, I visited with Archibald Hart, whose pioneering work on stress, contained in his book *Adrenaline and Stress,* looks at the biochemical results of the so-called "fight or flight" mechanism. As he pointed out in our conversation and in a luncheon address I heard him give, "Even good stress can kill you, because too much adrenaline for too long is bad for you whether it is caused by exciting challenges or tensions, fun or frustration, amusement or anxiety. My message is quite simple: The only stress that is good for you is the stress that is short lived!"[12] Hart noted that the distinction between healthy and unhealthy stress is a complicated one. We can't really determine the kind of stress we are experiencing by whether or not we enjoy what we are doing.

Without question, though, unhealthy stress can kill us. As we will see in chapter 3, stress is a major cause of heart disease, which is a leading cause of heart attacks. Other physical effects of stress range from migraine headaches to high blood pressure. The emotional effects of stress on the job can include depression or addictions to alcohol or prescription medication. Psychiatrists emphasize that the brain's natural antidotes to such things as depression become depleted under stress. Anxiety is heightened, and depression often follows. Stress has also been linked to many kinds of cancer and other diseases because it reduces the effectiveness of the body's immune system.

In our response to stress, we have begun to experience "adaptation," Hart said. He suggests that modern life has adapted many of us to a higher state of arousal. We've come to live with higher blood pressure and more adrenaline coursing through our veins. Our normal or "resting" level has increased significantly.[13] Part of the problem, Hart notes, is a frequent feeling of being out of control.

MIND AND BODY

Clearly how we respond to stress physically is important. However, it is equally important that body and mind respond to stress as a unit. Our mental responses, specifically our cognitive perceptions, must work with our body when stress comes. Several years ago, Chris Thurman, a Christian counselor and good friend, sat with me in a Fort Worth restaurant. After listening to my thoughts about stress and burnout, he pointed out, "Don, you're overlooking an important factor —cognitive perceptions. After all, Mark Twain once said, 'It's not so much what you eat that kills you, it's what eats you.'"

How we regard troublesome events will influence whether we feel stress much more than the events themselves warrant. Regard them as catastrophic, and high anxiety and stress will kick in. In many instances our feelings of loss of control—of overwhelming pressure—contribute significantly to the negative effects of stress. That's one reason I'm convinced that a thoroughly biblical and Christian approach to work-related stress is crucial.

My personal and vocational experience as a pastor, a radio counselor, and a conference speaker has convinced me of the ability of God's Word to change and renew our thinking. All of us can find ourselves distracted by the anxieties of life. Yet Peter reminds us to cast all our care on the Lord because He cares for us (1 Peter 5:7). An awareness that God is working in all things to produce ultimate good to those who love Him can guide and strengthen us when we feel that life is out of control (Romans 8:28). When the circumstances of work and life grow stressful, David's words can stabilize our thoughts and feelings: "Delight yourself also in the Lord, and He shall give you the desires of your heart. Commit your way to the Lord, trust also in Him, and He shall bring it to pass" (Psalm 37:4–5). So can Paul's reminder to "be anxious for nothing, but in everything by prayer . . . let your requests be known to God," as we focus our thoughts on those things that are good, honorable, and worthwhile (Philippians 4:6–10).[14]

If you have been saying to yourself or to others, "Help! My job is stressing me out," stay with us as we consider both practical insights into stress in the workplace and workable strategies for coping.

IT'S A RAT RACE OUT THERE

S everal years ago, as scientist L. K. Dahl and his colleagues conducted a series of studies on rats to determine the impact of salt on hypertension, they made another important discovery. They found that when the rats were exposed to certain kinds of stresses, their blood pressures rose significantly higher, even to potentially deadly levels.[1] Maybe you've heard someone say in jest, "It's a rat race out there, and the rats are winning." According to this study, the rats are losing too!

HISTORICAL PERSPECTIVE

Those of us who live in the rat race of the '90s don't have to read scientific or medical studies to realize that modern life, especially the workplace today, is incredibly stressful. But did you know that stressful situations date back to the earliest times? Adam, the first man on earth, was also the first farmer. God told him to expect thorns, thistles, and hard work for the rest of his life (Genesis 3:18–19), and so it has been ever since. We live by the sweat of our brow in most physical occupations, and most professionals will tell you that they, too, find hard study and work part of their job description.

Overwork and stress in the workplace are hardly modern phenomena. Throughout history, men have found working to be hard. Consider the Middle Ages, when people worked intensely for long hours just to eke out a living. Church reformer Martin Luther was born in the German village of Eisleben, where his father, John, worked as a poor woodcutter. Others in the community labored in the mines, and later in his life John Luther established two smelting furnaces in Mansfeldt —furnaces where Martin worked with his father.[2] Later John Luther became a city official in Mansfeldt. Luther's mother, Margaret, often carried wood on her back. Luther said, "They endured the severest labor for our sakes."

In the eighteenth century, many of the citizens of London labored long hours in factories under the harshest and most unsafe conditions. Children were sometimes crushed. In *A Tale of Two Cities* Charles Dickens describes the period as both the best and the worst of times. The work situation in the United States during that century and during much of the nineteenth century also was physically challenging. Many Americans lived in rural settings, and life on the farm was anything but easy. People labored in the fields from sunup to sundown, often for little income and with significant stress.

THE WORKPLACE TODAY

Clearly, ours is not the only generation to struggle with workplace stress. However, as detailed in chapter 1, many factors in today's workplace often raise the levels of stress to intolerable proportions. An article in *Newsweek* labeled the 1980s as the "work decade" and suggested that "amid the bustle of power breakfasts [and faxes and] appointments, there is a dirty little secret in the age of the office: stress. Our jobs are killing us."[3] According to an advertising agency survey, three-quarters of Americans say their jobs cause them stress.

Of course, the stresses of life are not confined to the workplace. An investigation by the *Dallas Morning News* showed how the stresses of modern life affect the citizens of

Dallas. Under a three-fourth-inch headline with the words "Stressed Out," reporter Jeffrey Weiss likened the entire city to a stressed-out individual. He listed a litany of problems contributing to fear and uncertainty for residents: major increases during the previous two years in child abuse cases (up 19 percent), violence-related police calls (climbing 48 percent), and violent crime (up 15 percent). In addition, drunken-driving arrests had increased 18 percent, and the number of people seeking professional counseling rose 20 percent.[4] About the only decline during the two-year period was in average wage levels; and residents surveyed had greater concern about unemployment.

Change and Stress

Workplace stress overlaps with the pressure found in urban living. The *Morning News* study pointed out another factor contributing to stress in modern life: change. More than a third of the customers of the Dallas water companies had either had their water cut off or had changed addresses during the past year—a 10 percent increase over the past two years.[5]

Similarly, the pressures resulting from job changes can be highly stressful. Although the U.S. workforce may not be quite as mobile as our perceptions might indicate, there is probably less lifetime employment with the same company—from entry-level to retirement—than ever before. Some of the changes are chosen; others are forced. Many baby boomers (and to a lesser extent, baby busters) have jumped from job to job to acquire new skills, higher salaries, and even new living locations. Each change brings stress about an uncertain future and new co-workers and surroundings. Among the forced job changes, leading the way is the corporate downsizing that has pushed thousands of workers out of companies where they wanted to stay.[6]

Workplace Violence

The Dallas report on violence mirrors an increase of violence, threatened and real, in the workplace. Though terrorist bombings remain unlikely and the exception, the fear of attacks similar to the Oklahoma City bombing remains (see chapter 1). Most violence in the workplace has been related to despondent or angry employees caught up in the pressures of their jobs or soured personal relationships. We will look at the extent and causes of workplace violence in chapter 3. But we cannot ignore it as a contributor to stress. In fact, murder has actually become the number-one cause of death for women in the workplace; for men it ranks third, behind machine-related mishaps and driving accidents.[7]

Changing Technology

Changing technology has compounded levels of stress in the workplace. Few would have predicted the drastic changes that have occurred in the work environment during this century, from the automobile engine that transports us to work to nuclear power to generate electricity (see the "Stress Test"). Today, accelerating technology has resulted in a new generation of computers every eighteen months. In the process of such change, stress increases. Even positive changes can be stressful!

There's the learning curve for major new technology. Just being trained for new computers and other technology takes up time that could otherwise be devoted to carrying out employees' job responsibilities. Some time ago I received a new computer, a top-of-the-line Gateway 2000 486 with all the latest software programs. It was far more powerful than my previous computer and had much greater capabilities. However, I found myself spending many frustrating hours learning how to use the computer and its software.

Meanwhile, at our office another computer proved faulty, causing frequent downtime. This added frustration for an entire department, which entered the responses mailed in by individuals from all over the world. Then we moved the entire ministry to a modern, newly renovated office building in suburban Lincoln. Such major moves, which come with their

 **STRESS TEST**

Technology, Change, and Stress

Rapid changes in this century have brought their share of stress our way. Think about some of the predictions made just a few decades ago. Consider the following comments by the experts, whose forecasts were incorrect. Can you guess who made the following statements?

1. *"Everything that can be invented, has been invented"* (said in 1899).

2. *"Radio has no future"* (said in the late nineteenth century).

3. *"It is an idle dream to imagine that automobiles will take the place of railways in the long-distance movement of passengers"* (1913).

4. *"Who ... wants to hear actors talk [in motion pictures]?"* (1927).

5. *"There is not the slightest indication that nuclear energy will ever be obtainable"* (1932).

6. *"There will never be enough problems, enough work for more than one or two of these computers."* (1950s).*

ANSWERS: 1. Charles Duell, director of the U.S. Patent Office; 2. Lord Kelvin, president of the British Royal Society; 3. The American Road Congress; 4. Movie mogul Harry Warner of Warner Brothers; 5. Albert Einstein; 6. Howard Aiken, the Harvard mathematics instructor who proposed the first true computer to IBM president Thomas Watson.

* Thomas Steinert-Threldkeld, "False Prophets and Bon Mots," *Dallas Morning News,* December 29, 1989.

own set of stressful situations, are happening more often in corporate America.

Longer Hours, Busier Hours

At one point modern technology was considered to be the solution for workplace stress—now it's more commonly recognized as part of the problem. Rather than freeing employees by letting them do more in less time, the fax machine, car phone, and beeper have caused the office to follow them everywhere, adding to the workload. My friend Mike, who started his own electronic service business, told me candidly one day, "Don, the technology is killing me. I'm in the middle of one project, and my beeper goes off. Someone else is having a problem with a system I've installed. I'm on my way to check on that, and the car phone rings with another problem. There are people calling me, leaving messages on my voice mail, asking for proposals—and they don't want them tomorrow—they want them faxed now!"

In her 1991 book *The Overworked American,* Harvard economist Juliet Schor estimated that the average U.S. worker is now putting in 164 more hours at paid labor per year than he or she did twenty years ago.[8] That's an extra month of work every year. Schor's figures cover vocations ranging from low-wage workers in fast-food restaurants, secretaries, and laborers to lawyers, doctors, and accountants.

Steady overtime has become a key factor in job stress as "corporate shrinkage" causes the workers who survive job cuts to carry heavier loads. According to workplace experts, employers are generally more cautious about hiring new employees because of the cost of such things as health benefits and training. They would prefer to work existing employees more, even at time-and-a-half, according to Virginia Guzman, an economist with the U.S. Department of Labor's Bureau of Labor Statistics. In the national manufacturing sector, workers averaged 5.1 hours of overtime weekly in September 1994. It was the highest unadjusted rate during the nineties.

Overtime can lead to job burnout and physical problems ranging from headaches to queasy stomachs or back and neck aches. On-the-job accident rates typically rise with overtime.[9]

Lower Wages

Declining real income, job changes, downsizing, and layoffs have often led to a shrinking salary picture. More and more workers feel overworked and underpaid at the same time. Although many companies are now prospering, statistics indicate that inflation-adjusted wages and benefits are climbing at less than half the pace of previous expansions, and a 1995 labor department survey shows that real employee compensation has actually been declining in recent years.[10]

Economists blame the decline on such factors as foreign job competition, technological changes, dwindling union influence, increased use of temporary help, and the massive downsizing in the defense sector. The result is far less real income for most workers, as salaries shrink and inflation climbs. For example, the average price of a car rose more than 70 percent during the past decade, while incomes increased only 40 percent.[11]

Temporary Employment

The trend in the '90s, to have more part-time workers and fewer full-time employees, saves costs in employee benefits and allows employee levels to flex according to demands in the industry. Unfortunately, it creates major uncertainty for employees, some of whom cannot count on employers for such simple things as medical coverage and paid sick time. How pervasive is the trend toward temporary employment? According to one survey, the number of temporary employment agencies has doubled during the past five years, from 3,500 companies in 1989 to more than 7,000 in 1994. These days, companies employ temporaries at every level of work, from entry level to management.[12]

The availability of faxes and computer modems means that employers don't even have to supply office space for temporary or even permanent office employees. Working out of their homes, they have no face or voice at the office, which reduces both their input and feedback ("Am I doing the job right?") and their sense of camaraderie and morale as an employee ("Does anyone care about me?").

THREE CONTRIBUTING FACTORS

Three factors seem to play a prominent role in the way modern life contributes to stress in the workplace: the full-time working mom, the midlife crisis, and financial pressures in general.

The Working Mom

A recent *Redbook* survey of nearly thirteen hundred working women indicated that one of the major sources of stress for working moms is trying to balance competing time demands. More than 70 percent of those surveyed felt that their husbands didn't do what they considered to be a fair share of housework—things such as cleaning, preparing meals, washing dishes, bathing and dressing children, and taking kids to doctors' appointments.[13] When moms have to balance those pressures with what they're facing at work, it's no wonder things seem overwhelming. (This issue is so crucial, we'll look at it in more detail in the next chapter.)

Some time ago I talked with a pastor friend about this problem. He suggested, "Well, why don't they just quit their jobs and become stay-at-home moms?" I pointed out that, although many of us might consider the ideal to be a two-parent family with dad working and mom home-schooling the 2.3 children, and both parents sharing cheerfully in the dinner dishes, that is not the usual situation. More than 50 percent of women work outside the home either part- or full-time. I'm convinced that we need to minister to people where they are, not where they should be.

The financial contribution many working women make to the household budget is significant. According to the *Redbook* survey, 33 percent indicated that their income accounts for between a quarter to a half of the total family income.

Although many moms have joined the workforce to pay for big-ticket options, such as a new car, boat, or furniture, more working women have found their second income essential to feed and clothe their children, since the average cost of raising a child to age seventeen now stands at $210,000 for median income families.[14]

My co-workers Tonya and Linda have wrestled with these issues. Linda is a single mom who had to raise her children while working outside the home; during our interview, Tonya was expecting her first child in only three months. "God just gives you grace for what you have to do," Linda said.

Mother-to-be Tonya recalled attending graduate school, losing another job when the boss/owner retired, and receiving her current position. "At this point I see how God has opened this door. Now that I'm expecting a baby, I don't think He's telling me that He's closing these doors just because I'm moving into the motherhood phase of life. I believe that the two phases can exist simultaneously.

"My husband and I are in agreement. In fact, he's no couch potato. He probably does more around the house than I do. We wrestled with the decision, how it would affect those around us, our families, our authorities at work, all those issues. The point is," Tonya continued, "it's just stressful to be a working mom. I have no illusions about that. I think every individual has to make her own decision, using common sense, seeking God's will, asking advice from other people and using wisdom. You have to determine what the will of God is. There's nothing like being in the will of God, and nobody else can tell you what the will of God for you is. As long as you are not doing something that the Bible specifically tells you not to do, and if husband and wife are in agreement, then I think you make the decision from there."

Midlife Crisis

The stresses associated with midlife changes for women have been well documented, but only in recent years has the term "midlife crisis" been used to describe a key source of heightened stress for men. According to Christian counselor Jim Conway, "Of all the stages and transitions a man goes through in adulthood, it appears that the mid-life crisis is the most dangerous and painful for him, his family and the community."[15] It's a time when many people begin asking themselves the question posed by a popular song of several decades ago: "Is that all there is?"

It often happens during a period identified by popular author Gail Sheehy as "the deadline decade," "the years between ages thirty-five to forty-five,"[16] when people wrestle with questions such as: Who am I? Is what I'm doing meaningful? Do I want to do this for the rest of my life? Do I even want to continue being who I am? Sometimes sudden, precipitous job changes can occur. Stress is at an all-time high and contentment at an all-time low.

It's also a time when many men and women are tempted to engage in extramarital affairs, a source of incredible stress and significant consequences both at work and at home, as a recent letter to advice columnist Abigail Van Buren indicates:

> *Dear Abby:*
> *I am a man who has been married for more than twenty years, but I, like many others, lacked something in my marriage. I found that something in a woman with whom I worked. "Anna" also lacked something in her marriage. We fell in love and became intimate... but our affair was discovered.... I made a terrible mistake.... There are no words to describe the hurt I feel.... My wife hasn't thrown me out, but she freezes up if I even put my arm around her.... I'd like to offer a message to other men: Please don't cheat on your wife. Keep your mind on your work, not on a female coworker."[17]*

Incidentally, moral failures are not limited to those in midlife. Christians of all ages are warned, "Let him who thinks he stands take heed lest he fall" (1 Corinthians 10:12). Actually, midlife can and should be a time of productive self-evaluation—reestablishing priorities and finding meaning and fulfillment even in the routines of life. So much depends on how we handle it.

Financial Crunch

One factor that often lies at the heart of pressure on the working wife and mother or the working husband who feels trapped in midlife crisis is the overwhelming financial crunch of life today. According to many authorities, the '90s represent the first decade since World War II when individuals cannot expect a higher standard of living than the previous generation. According to the *Redbook* survey conducted by Deborah Belle of Boston University, money pressures rated even higher than job-related issues as generating the most stress in life: 43 percent of respondents rated money the greatest source of stress, compared to 27 percent for work.[18]

Earning a living is the main motivation behind our work; the paycheck should be important to us. Yet what is the priority in spending our income if we want to honor God? Let's take a quick look at two important New Testament passages for a biblical perspective on finances.

Jesus' parable about talents (Matthew 25:14–27) came on the heels of an extended warning He gave about the time leading up to His return, a time in which we seem to be living today. He described a businessman traveling to a distant country who entrusted a variety of talents, or sums of money, to his servants: five to one, two to another, one to a third, to each according to his ability.

From this parable we can recognize several key principles. First, our finances are not our own; they are actually a trust we've been given from God. Second, God wants us to exercise faithfulness with them, not fall into the trap of financial competitiveness. Third, based on the uses these three men made of their resources—two traded for additional benefits while the third hid his money in the ground—I conclude that God wants us to use our money to benefit Him, not just ourselves. Fourth, we will gain some benefit from hard work and wise use of financial resources in this life; there is hope for personal advancement. However, our reward ultimately comes in heaven, not here on earth. Finally, the way we handle our money—how we earn it, how we spend it, save it, or give it—has a great deal to say about our relationship with God and the development of our faith in Him.

The apostle Paul wrote to Timothy, a young pastor, giving him a formula for financial success—the kind of thing so many people either seek or claim to have today. Paul's reminder that godliness plus contentment equals great gain provides the ultimate key to handling our finances. Like Jesus, Paul reminds us that all we have and are ultimately comes from God Himself (1 Timothy 6:7). Thus, we are to feel content just to have our basic needs met (v. 8). Those who have a strong resolve to become rich will ultimately experience pain, stress, and destruction (v. 9), since the love of money is the root of all kinds of evil, spiritually and otherwise (v. 10).

Instead of seeking after money, Paul urges Timothy to pursue such character virtues as righteousness, godliness, faith, love, patience, and gentleness (v. 11). He further charges those who do possess wealth not to be proud or trust in their uncertain riches but rather to rely on God, cultivate an attitude of thankfulness, practice generosity, and live with eternal, rather than temporal, values in view (vv. 17–19).

Since there is so much in Scripture about money and how to deal with it, it seems that one of the most important ways we can reduce stress in the workplace is by developing a proper biblical understanding and approach to our personal finances.

THE CHRISTIAN WORKPLACE

Before we move on to look at the shattering impact of workplace stress, let me take a moment to dispel a widely held myth—that somehow working for a Christian organization guarantees a stress-free workplace.

Stress is a major component in the lives of pastors and missionaries. It is a major factor in people's leaving the ministry. Frequently we deny or refuse to discuss the issue because of the idealistic image we may have of those in ministry. My friend Walter DeSmet, who has encountered a wide range of stresses, including the death of his wife, wrote:

> *The missionary often finds himself walking a tightrope. If he comes across too negatively, he is branded as a failure. If, on the other hand, he's always positive, he may be accused of being less than truthful. The missionary is not exempt from stress. In fact, the problem may be much bigger than most of us realize.*[19]

Meanwhile, many church members believe that the pastor, as "God's representative," will always do everything just right. Typically, pastors are on call twenty-four hours a day, and those in smaller churches do not have anyone to "cover for them" the way pastors in larger, multistaffed churches do. As a former senior pastor, I've seen how staff members can have conflicts with each other, how churches can experience division and conflict as well as healing and growth, and how building programs can be extremely stressful for leaders trying to carry on the normal responsibilities plus the building program with its added time and financial demands.

In addition, job security can be just as much an issue in the pastorate as in the secular workplace. A 1988 survey by the Southern Baptist Sunday School Board showed that more than 2,100 pastors had been dismissed by their churches during the previous eighteen months.[20] This survey indicated that an average of 116 churches and pastors severed their relationships through involuntary termination every month, a 31 percent increase over a 1984 survey. Such terminations didn't happen just because of moral failures or financial misconduct. Almost 45 percent were over subjective issues such as performance dissatisfaction, authoritarian leadership style, power struggles, and personality conflicts. Only 5 percent were dismissed over doctrinal issues and just over 3 percent for family problems. More than 25 percent of the pastors terminated had been fired more than once.

In 2 Corinthians, the apostle Paul wrote at length about stress in the ministry. He spoke of the press of his daily "deep concern for all the churches" (11:28) and described the pressure that had at one point caused him to despair "even of life" (1:8). He reminded those to whom he wrote that, since ministry is a trust from God, we must never give up (4:1).

In short, the Christian workplace, though viewed by many as idyllic, is filled with most of the same stresses faced by workers in any other environment, plus a few that are unique to this particular kind of organization. Missionaries experience such stresses as extended travel, living in a different culture, learning a foreign language, and struggling to communicate even in the simplest of ways. Pastors and Christian counselors face the stress of listening to the hurts and pains of others hour after hour, responding with compassion, yet not allowing what they hear to affect their own marriages and family relationships. It is important for those of us who are part of church families to recognize the importance of providing emotional as well as financial and spiritual support for those involved in vocational ministries.

No doubt about it, it's a rat race out there. Even so, let's remember that we aren't rats; we are people created in the image of God, designed to show His glory to those around us. One way we can do that is to learn how to handle the stresses that life throws at us, whether financial, interpersonal, or vocational. Taking action to deal with our stresses appropriately can restore meaning, balance, and contentment to our lives.

CHAPTER THREE

WHAT STRESS DOES TO US

S ome time ago, after I had spoken on the effects of stress at a pastors' conference, I talked with two pastors who held opposing views about the impact of stress. One cited an article from the Mayo Clinic that suggested as much as 90 percent of all visits to a physician involved stress-related illnesses. The other called my approach to stress "doom and gloom" and added, "There's no point in making stress the scapegoat for all these bad things. After all, I'd rather burn out for God than rust out. I think you need to quit talking so much about stress and talk more about commitment, dedication, and perseverance."

The comments of the two ministers reminded me of our need to be balanced in our approach to these issues. Still, we must recognize how serious the implications of stress can be and the shattering impact that workplace stress can have, not just on our work performance but on our personal health, on our relationships, indeed on every aspect of our lives.

Several months before my conversation with the two ministers, I spoke to a group of missionaries in Europe on burnout. Their initial reaction echoed the words of the second pastor. The problem, according to most missionaries there, was not that they were burning out or needed to slow down. Instead, as one suggested, I needed to go back to the United States and tell the Christians there to show the same kind of commitment and effort they were demonstrating in their ministry. Yet, within a few days, that missionary and his colleagues had all recognized the stress and burnout manifested in their own lives, families, and ministries. They were ready to deal with some of the issues of stress.

BEYOND DENIAL

Often that's where we find ourselves, needing to move past denial, beyond the fact that we don't feel stressed out. Our marriages may seem satisfactory, and we haven't had a heart attack, so we think stress has little effect on our lives. What's actually happened is that we have become conditioned to a more hurried, stress-filled lifestyle (see page 27).

In all likelihood, you are under stress in the workplace. A few years ago, seven of every ten respondents to a survey by Northwestern National Life Insurance Company labeled job stress the single greatest strain in their lives. They said it lowered their productivity at work and caused frequent physical ailments, and 72 percent said they averaged three or more stress-related conditions at work every week—anger, anxiety, headaches, muscle pain, insomnia, or exhaustion.

An article in the February 1, 1995, issue of the *Wall Street Journal* reported that job stress "is corrosive to family members and their well-being. . . . According to the Families and Work Institute of New York, job stress is more than three times more likely to spill over into the home than family problems are to crop up at work."[1] The *Journal* noted the special impact of stress on single parents, recounting how Veronica, a single mother with one son, held down two part-time jobs. As a bookkeeper and a parking control officer, she received no paid time off, and her bosses had repeatedly turned down her applications to become a permanent, full-time employee, even though they had told her she does good work. For Veronica, even routine incidents can heighten stress levels. When her four-year-old son fell off the monkey bars at day care, she was forced to leave work to take him to the doctor. The incident cost her most of a day's pay—and left her feeling significantly stressed out.

HAZARDOUS TO YOUR HEALTH

Workers at one Midwest firm found themselves spontaneously laughing one morning as they clocked in. Pinned to the bulletin board over the time clock was a large sign, placed there surreptitiously and unofficially: "Warning: Working here may be hazardous to your health." In fact, the list of stress-related maladies that cause worker absenteeism or physical problems reads like the index of a medical textbook. This should not be surprising, as the Scriptures note that spirit, soul, and body are clearly linked together—what affects one, affects all (1 Thessalonians 5:23).

Struggling with emotional pressures will create physical problems, and physical pain will lead to emotional and spiritual problems. An estimated 50 to 70 percent of those who visit a general or family practice physician are there primarily because of a stress-related problem.[2] Without question, being overworked and stressed-out from our jobs is affecting the level of our health and well-being in general.

Thus, headaches are often associated with workplace stress. According to Ed Blanchard, professor of psychology at the State University of New York at Albany, stress is a major cause of tension headaches, the most common type, and of migraines as well.[3] Just think of all the products invented to deal with the kind of pain caused by headaches: aspirin, buffered aspirin, Tylenol® (which contains acetaminophen), Motrin® (which contains ibuprofen), and numerous other generic and brand-name medications.

A second major health issue affected by stress is heart disease. According to medical authorities, both high blood pressure and elevated blood cholesterol levels can result from increased stress. Several physicians I've talked with tell me that stress itself doesn't cause heart disease, but once a person has heart disease, stress will significantly increase his chances of dying from it.

Many authorities point out that a high percentage of heart attacks occur before 9:00 A.M. Most of us tend to believe that people get tired and have a heart attack at the end of the day. But it may be that the stress of getting out of bed and facing work in the morning—perhaps a dreaded job—is enough to bring on a heart attack.

Furthermore, as my personal physician reminded me at my last checkup, stress can actually cause an elevation in the "bad cholesterol" that often leads to clogged arteries and heart problems. He pointed out that several studies found that people who perform mentally stressful activities, such as income tax preparers and certified public accountants experience a temporary rise in cholesterol just before the April 15 tax deadline.

Stress also can affect the digestive system. According to the *Wall Street Journal,* stress in the workplace has made the antacid market massive, grossing between $800 million and $1 billion per year.[4] Drug giant SmithKline Beecham saw its stock jump significantly when it persuaded the Food and Drug Administration to approve an over-the-counter version of Tagamet®, its widely used prescription medication for ulcers. SmithKline already sells Tums®, one of the most popular over-the-counter antacids.

One common stress-related digestive ailment today is irritable bowel syndrome (IBS). Most of us experience some kind of gastrointestinal distress on occasion, usually from a combination of unfamiliar food or water and stress. However, physicians indicate that frequent problems such as abdominal pain, cramping, bloating, diarrhea, and/or constipation may indicate irritable bowel syndrome. Some medical authorities estimate that IBS affects one in every ten adults. There is no known cause or cure for IBS, and it usually can't

 **STRESS TEST**

The Top Five Stress Producers

The stress survey of *Redbook* magazine readers (see chapter 2) found several work factors that readers said created stress for them. Below are the top five. Put a check mark in front of any of these you are experiencing. (The percent in parentheses after each statement indicates the percentage of survey respondents who experienced these factors.)

☐ 1. *My work duties are repetitive in nature (71 percent).*

☐ 2. *Work leaves me feeling exhausted (61 percent).*

☐ 3. *I don't have enough time left for family concerns after returning home from work (44 percent).*

☐ 4. *My job feels like a dead end, with no opportunity for advancement (35 percent).*

☐ 5. *It's difficult to get time off to tend to my children's needs and appointments (19 percent).*

be detected by physical exam. Some studies have indicated that irritable bowel syndrome patients are more susceptible to the effects of stress than others.[5]

Another, perhaps more serious, digestive issue involves ulcers. At one point the medical community thought stress caused ulcers by triggering excess stomach acid. Now, however, many physicians believe that a specific bacterial species in the system called helicobacterpylori is the main factor for duodenal, or small intestine, ulcers and about three-fourths of all stomach ulcers.[6]

Workplace stress is a contributing factor in a wide range of additional illnesses, including everything from diabetes to cancer, plus emotional illnesses ranging from depression to anxiety disorders and addictions. One study at the University of California in Los Angeles showed that people who have a history of on-the-job aggravation over a ten-year period face more than five times the risk of colon and rectal cancer as those with little or no stress at work.[7]

SIDETRACKED BY STRESS

How stress combines to drain us physically and emotionally is demonstrated in the life of a corporate executive for a large pizza chain. Bruce Neuharth was on an upward career track as a manager for the Pizza Hut Corporation. As he put it, "My commitment to building a career caused a lot of stress for me, but I actually enjoyed it. I gained a reputation with our company as the man to call on to send into an area where restaurants were struggling. Life was a continual pressure cooker for me, but I relished that."[8]

Before long the stress started taking an increased physical toll. Neuharth began drinking heavily to relieve the pressures of the day. Physical and medical problems developed, including a deteriorating hip socket. "For a while I thought all I needed was a change of scenery," he said. Serious intestinal problems, continued bouts with alcohol, plus a marriage on the rocks all helped bring Neuharth to turn in faith to Christ. "My decision to become a Christian did not immediately solve my problems. Because my bone structure had continued to deteriorate, I had to undergo . . . a total hip replacement. But my marriage and my family life improved dramatically. Although I still greatly enjoy my work, I began to see how much I had neglected my wife and children."

Now the director for training and development for Godfathers Pizza, Bruce still faces on-the-job stress. "The difference is how I deal with it. In the past I would keep it bottled up until I reached a breaking point, try to drown the stress with several drinks, or just not handle it at all, allowing the situation to boil over into uncontrolled anger. Now I turn to God, praying for his wisdom and insight."[9]

There's another negative impact of workplace stress, and it's often communicable. According to David Cooney, president of Goodwill Industries International, stress can actually be communicated to those around us. Cooney points out that, in small quantities, stress can stimulate us and make us creative. In excessive amounts, however, it reduces our effectiveness.[10] It's not that stress is communicable in the same way we can catch a disease such as a cold, from a virus or a bacterium. Yet one stressed-out individual can actually raise the stress level of others by his or her responses.

Cooney suggests that stress not only can make us physically ill and affect those around us, it can also paralyze us, causing virtual inaction or even terribly inappropriate actions when we face important choices. Thus, it can be hazardous even to our careers.

PAINFUL WORK

Safety in the workplace concerns people in a variety of work environments. According to the National Safety Council, 3.3 million workers suffered disabling accidents in 1992; from those accidents, 8,500 workers died, including 1,700 government workers, 1,300 construction workers, 1,300 service-industry workers, and 1,200 in both the agricultural and transportation/public utilities areas. The disabling injuries affected almost every area of the body, with the top areas being the back (800,000 workers) and leg (440,000 workers).[11]

Carpal tunnel syndrome, which creates pain in the wrist and arms of many who enter data on computers, is a distinct occupational hazard of the computerized '90s. Improper positioning of the hands, shoulders, and even the back at the keyboard is often blamed. Susan is a secretary-typist in a large corporate office, but an ongoing problem with carpal tunnel has made it almost impossible for her to use her considerable typing skills. Carpal tunnel syndrome is one of a series of degenerative problems often referred to as cumulative trauma disorders, or CTDs, that now leaves many secretaries, telephone operators, data-listing clerks, and assembly-line workers with damaged muscles, tendons, and joints.

Alex has worked in a chemical plant for a number of years but has developed asthma, most likely as a result of exposure to toxic fumes in the lab. Marj, who was fired from her job at an electronics firm because of excessive absence due to health problems, developed pneumonia, liver damage, and gall bladder disease from long-term exposure to potent chemicals at work.

KILLER WORK

A 1993 survey by Northwestern National Life Insurance reported that more than two million employees suffer physical attacks on the job each year, and more than six million are threatened in some way.[12] Those run the gamut from death threats phoned to CEOs' homes to workers speaking of mass murder and specifying which guns they'll use on which supervisors.

According to experts, the problem isn't just the violence in society as a whole. An increasingly harsh, stressful work environment, plus the ongoing wave of layoffs, have left workers feeling dispensable and threatened with finding jobs with lower pay, less benefits, and little or no job satisfaction. A recent *Time/CNN* poll reported that 37 percent of Americans see workplace violence as a growing problem.[13]

According to the National Institute for Occupational Safety and Health, homicide has become the third leading cause of work-related deaths in the United States.[14] Up until late 1992, an average of only one employer-directed homicide per month was committed in the United States. Today the body count averages five or six per month.

Over the past decade, postal workers, after being laid off or having disagreements at several post offices, have come to work with firearms and wreaked havoc: thirty-four postal employees have been murdered by co-workers and twenty-six wounded. Police and postal management suspect that the pressures of the job (including long hours, complaining customers, and crowded facilities) contributed to the violence.

"It used to be we went to work to earn a living," management consultant Dennis Johnson told a conference on workplace violence hosted by the Postal Service. "Today, frequently, we go to the workplace to die or to be killed."[15] The meeting on workplace violence was the outgrowth of ten recent major incidents of post office violence.[16]

Ironically, that meeting opened the same day a teacher shot to death a school principal and wounded another principal and a teacher at a high school in Chelsea, Michigan. Two days earlier, four pizza workers had been shot to death in Aurora, Colorado. Just a few days later, a post office holdup in suburban Montclair, New Jersey, left four people dead and a fifth critically wounded.[17] According to Montclair Police Chief Thomas Russo, two of the victims were postal employees and two were customers.

In addition to the causes cited by investigators of Postal Service violence, we can include disagreements among coworkers. A Federal Express pilot attacked three fellow crew members with a claw hammer in the cockpit of a DC-10 over a disagreement; a purchasing manager in a suburban Chicago office stabbed his boss to death because the two couldn't agree on how to handle paperwork. And a North Carolina technician quit his job because he had trouble working for a woman, then sneaked back inside the fiber optics laboratory and began firing a semiautomatic pistol. He killed two and injured two more before he turned the gun on himself.[18]

Workplace violence is even taking its toll in the supposedly tranquil heartland. In rural Schuyler, Nebraska, a man with a history of assaulting his former common-law wife shot her and her new boyfriend to death before killing himself in the parking lot of a meatpacking plant. The plant had been the scene of earlier violence. In November 1989, a man and woman were shot and killed as they arrived at work. The woman's estranged husband was sentenced to two consecutive life prison terms in that incident. Three Michigan shooting incidents, all involving active employees at different automobile plants, led to the deaths of five Michigan auto factory workers since September 1994. And a triple murder and suicide occurred at a plant in Columbus, Nebraska, about twenty miles west of Schuyler.[19]

Violence in the workplace now costs U.S. employers more than $4 billion per year, according to a study by the National Safe Workplace Institute. An estimated 111,000 violent incidents occurred in the work environment in 1992 alone.[20] According to psychologist Dennis Johnson, president of Behavior Analysts and Consultants in Florida, which gathers statistics on workplace violence, the typical workplace killer is a man who is probably a loner, frustrated by problems at work, and with few relationships away from the job.

Then there is the issue of safety from terrorism, especially in the aftermath of the Oklahoma City bombing. Though bombings remain a rarity among causes of workplace violence, many companies have recognized the need to develop a workplace violence prevention program. Gary Mathiason, a San Francisco lawyer who has designed several such programs, estimates that one in six American companies (17 percent) have violence prevention plans. He believes that the total could reach three of every four U.S. companies within five years. Security for child care facilities also has become a major issue. According to Joseph Kinney, executive director of the National Safe Workplace Institute in Chicago, violence directed against employers or former employers is the fastest growing category of workplace violence.[21]

BALANCING THE FAMILY

The stresses at work often are matched by stresses at home, especially for those workers who are also parents. For female employees, the pressure to balance work and family has reached such crisis proportion that one Dallas psychiatrist has labeled such anxiety "female executive stress syndrome." That shouldn't be surprising when, as one popular commercial put it, the woman goes out to "bring home the bacon," then returns home to "fry it up in a pan."

The pressures on women executives who thought they could "have it all" by combining work and family have led to major life losses and even severe depression, according to a study by researcher Sylvia Gearing.[22] She concluded that women may feel in control inside the office, but outside the work arena many of them feel that things are falling apart. Those with careers, family, and even a big salary, feel overwhelmed by stresses. *Fortune* magazine estimates that 40 percent of today's managers and administrators are women.

Although Gearing's conclusions may be suspect (she urges a return to the feminist movement as a solution), she has identified a legitimate area of stress. Many women have become workaholics, more comfortable at the office than at home, perfectionists who are never happy with their performance. Some have even cut off their feminine sides in order to battle it out in male-dominated workplaces. Driven by fear, they withdraw from intimacy with family or friends.

According to a Massachusetts Mutual Insurance survey, Americans believe that "parents having less time to spend with their families is the single most important reason for the family's decline in our society."[23] When *Fortune* published an article titled "Is Your Company Asking Too Much?" the response from corporate executives was, in effect, "You ain't seen nothing yet." A recent Lou Harris poll found that the average workweek had increased from 40.6 hours in 1973 to 46.6 hours in 1987. For professional people, the average was 52 hours per week, with an average of 57 hours per week for corporate executives and small business owners.[24]

Without question, the family takes a major hit from such time demands. The volatile combination of work stress and less family time leads to a variety of problems ranging from children who feel alienated to marital breakdown and divorce.

According to Margaret Fong of Memphis State University, professional single women are particularly at risk because of the lack of a supportive partner and the stress of being defined by what they are not—unmarried or childless.[25] She reports that these women often show higher levels of illness, stress symptoms, and even depression.

So, how can parents win this war and achieve balance? Psychologist Mortimer Feinberg suggests using what the medical community calls the "triage method." Rather than trying to solve all the balancing problems at once, sit down with your spouse and decide which ones need immediate attention and which can wait. Feinberg recommends always trying to reach agreement on important issues, even if it means putting off decisions on some others.[26]

Other practical responses include negotiating with your boss for less work time, seeking help from your personnel or employee relations department, or even asking for permission to work full- or part-time at home—an increasingly popular alternative in an age of modems and fax machines.

Another significant strategy we can all use to help balance work and family is to lower expectations. In *How to Beat Burnout,* my coauthors and I identified high expectations as one of the key factors leading to both personal and job burnout. So many times our expectations wind up in conflict, especially when we expect to totally succeed with every project at work, be the perfect spouse, provide all our children with quality time, and still earn a comfortable living.

Perhaps the commercials were wrong. Maybe we can't "have it all." So instead of trying, let's readjust those targets and scale back our expectations. Who knows? In the process we may begin to resolve some of the family conflict, head off marital breakups, lower the possibility of responding to stress and pain with personal addictions, cut down on job absenteeism, and enhance our personal physical, emotional, and even spiritual well-being. In doing those things, we ultimately will lower the shattering impact of workplace stress.

CHAPTER FOUR

BACK TO EDEN: WHERE WORK BEGAN

I 'm not sure why you'd want to have a Bible study on *work*,"
Art said as he poured coffee into a cup, then stirred in arti-
ficial sweetener and creamer. "You're the pastor, but it seems
to me that what we really need is to study doctrine—or maybe prophecy, since the world is in such bad shape."

"I appreciate your perspective, Art," I replied.

I remembered a discussion Art and I had over lunch a few
weeks before. He had insisted that the subject of work was
part of what he considered the secular arena. An earnest,
hard-driving man in his mid-thirties, Art was part of a family
business founded and run by his dad. Art and his two brothers, who were also part of the business, had all acquired their
father's sense of drivenness. Art and his family were faithful
in church attendance, and Art himself was keenly interested
in studying things such as Bible doctrine and prophecy. It
seemed to me from several of our conversations that his work
and his spiritual life didn't often mix.

Cindy had just finished doctoring her coffee with a massive
amount of powdered creamer. Now she chimed in. "Frankly,
Pastor Don, I think the whole subject of work is a futile one
anyway. Maybe the Bible does talk about it, but I'm not sure

what the Bible could have to say to make me feel any better about waiting tables at Denny's. I mean, I need my job, and it helps me support my kids, but I don't ever expect working tables to turn into any kind of utopia."

I couldn't help smiling as I thought about how I had planned to introduce our discussion by pointing out that work began in the Garden of Eden. It just might be a challenge to convince people like Cindy, who encountered all kinds of stressful situations waiting tables, or like Rich, who spent his working hours in the greasy world of an automobile mechanic, that there was anything Edenic about work. For them, stress was part of the job, God was involved but little, and they did not know how, from a biblical perspective, they could "enjoy" their work.

The discussion we had planned on work was part of a series of forums designed to acquaint people in the church with what I felt were some of the critical issues facing believers in our stress-filled world. We had already addressed spiritual life in general and how the Bible applies to marriages and parenting. Still ahead were discussions on witnessing and Bible prophecy.

"Don't get me wrong, pastor," Art said. "These discussions are a great idea. I am just not sure how work fits."

THE BIBLE AND WORK

Art raised a valid question, one with direct implications for the subject of this book. After all, if the subject of work is strictly limited to the secular arena, if it resulted from the Fall, and if God has very little to say about it, then there was little point in holding a forum on the issue or even spending time examining the subject in the Bible.

However, I had become convinced that Scripture has a lot to say about our work, since God introduced work to our original parents before sin ever entered the world. God's desire was to provide meaning, purpose, and needed structure for our lives through work and to use our work to fulfill His purposes. I wanted a cross section of individuals to discuss the topic, and the group of church members who had signed up to participate was fairly diverse.

Ralph had been a carpenter for many years. In fact, he had worked on both building and maintenance projects at church. On several occasions we had talked about the insecurities of construction work. "You have to take it when it comes," Ralph said. "It's sort of feast-or-famine. I may be making good money on a project for a few months. Then— *bang*—the project's over. There's nothing else to do, and I can go weeks or even months without working."

Vern, on the other hand, probably could afford to go without working. He **owned several companies**, which he had built by long hours and hard work. Now, close to retirement age, he had hired a manager to oversee his various business interests, but he still put in what most people would call an average day at the office.

Deena was a therapist, whose work involved helping individuals resolve conflicts and problems at work, home, and in their personal lives.

David was an educator dealing with the particular stresses of public high school. He taught English, math, and music; in this final field he often encountered irate parents who believed that their son or daughter hadn't received the recognition they really deserved for outstanding talents.

Like Vern, **Lynn owned her own business**—a furniture and appliance dealership that she personally had run since her husband died three years earlier. She was a friendly, outgoing woman with a perpetual smile and a no-nonsense approach to business affairs.

They, along with **Rich the mechanic**, **Cindy the waitress**, and **Art the family-business co-owner**, constituted my "workplace discussion group." Their differences of opinion surfaced when I introduced my first question: "Do we work because of the Fall?"

"Absolutely," David insisted. "It's right there in Genesis 3:17–19. God told Adam the ground was cursed after he sinned, and he'd eat by the sweat of his face."

Looking around, I noticed several heads nodding agreement. Somehow I had suspected that the view that work originated with the Fall was a common one—that Adam and Eve had actually been destined to enjoy the long-term equivalent of an exotic Caribbean or South Sea island vacation with nothing more to do than stroll through the Garden, relax by the pool, or admire the beauty of God's creation.

Before the Fall

In my response to David I noted that work actually originated before the Fall. In fact, work is the very first subject addressed in Scripture, I told the group. The project described was a massive one and involved incredible creativity. The work of creation took place over a period of six days, and it was carried out by God Himself.

"In the beginning God created the heavens and the earth" (Genesis 1:1). "So the first point to consider," I explained, "is that work preceded the Fall. The Fall did have an impact on it, but work existed before sin entered God's creation."

The subject of the very first sentence in the Bible is "God." The verb, which indicates His action, is "created"; the direct object, the focus of His creativity, is "the heavens and the earth." Years in the ministry, teaching and preaching God's Word, have long ago convinced me of the value of learning the meaning, identity, and relationship of the different parts of speech. And right here, in the beginning of the biblical record, that significance comes into play. The Lord God Himself took action. He created. The Hebrew verb means exactly what the English suggests—creativity. In fact, the word *bara,* which is used in Genesis 1:1, and again in 2:7 to describe the formation of man from the dust of the ground, stresses the newness and perfection of what is created, and it is used in the Bible only with God as its subject.[1]

 **STRESS TEST** . . . .

Jobs, Jobs, Jobs

Many Christians believe they should rarely change jobs, as they believe God called them to their postions. However, being "called to a job" simply means that in any one job I can sense that my work has meaning and dignity and gives me an opportunity to serve God and people while I earn a living.

If you believe that your skills and talents are not being used fully or being further developed, or that your income needs are not being met (minimal raises in the past two years), it may be time to consider a new job. God does not necessarily ask you to stay at the same company. A new job will create stresses of its own, but that may be better than the mounting pressures of a job that does not satisfy.

Others feel that their job is not sufficiently service-oriented and could not please God. But any job God gives you will benefit others in some way. The Bible sanctions job variety and changes. There is freedom to make a change, even a change for the better, if God permits.

Identify the variety of occupations held by these Bible figures:

1. *Cain was a* _____ *(Genesis 4:2).*   2. *Abel was a* _____ *(4:2).*   3. *Aaron was a* _____ *(Exodus 28:1).*   4. *Miriam was a* _____ *(15:20–21).*   5. *Bezaleel and Aholiab were* _____ *(31:3–6).*   6. *Amos the prophet was a* _____ *(Amos 7:14).*   7. *Joab was a* _____ *(2 Samuel 8:16).*   8. *Lydia was a* _____ *(Acts 16:14).*   9. *Zacchaeus was a* _____ *(Luke 19:2).*   10. *Priscilla, Aquila, and Paul were* _____ *(Acts 18:2–3).*

ANSWERS: 1. farmer, a tiller of the ground; 2. keeper of sheep (shepherd); 3. priest; 4. leader in worship; 5. skilled artisans and craftsmen; 6. herdsman and a gatherer of sycamore figs; 7. military commander; 8. merchant selling textiles; 9. tax collector; 10. tentmakers.

. . . .

Invented by God

Several observations grow out of the fact that creative work was both invented and modeled by God Himself.

First, work is intrinsically good, not inherently evil. After all, the view of God presented in Scripture is one of absolute holiness and righteousness. The apostle John describes God as "light, and in Him there is no darkness at all" (1 John 1:5). The implication seems crystal clear: the one who initiated work is God. He created the universe in which we live; thus, work cannot be inherently bad, since it originated in Him.

Second, God observed and evaluated everything He had made and labeled it "very good" (Genesis 1:31). Just think of all God included in that evaluation—the beautiful stars, the incredible expanse of heaven, the sky and clouds, sparkling seas, grass, fruit trees, flowers, the brilliant sun ruling by day, the "lesser light" of the moon shining through the night, a vast variety of living creatures—from small to massive sea creatures filling the waters to birds flying across the skies and cattle and wild animals roaming the earth. Finally man appeared, Adam and his wife, Eve, the capstone of God's creation, taking their place of dominion and bearing the image —the nature and attributes—of God Himself.

Third, God did not create man simply to resemble Him but to reflect His image and likeness. The active purpose for man was to "have dominion" (Genesis 1:26), a purpose God clearly explained as He blessed them and said, "Be fruitful and multiply; fill the earth and subdue it; have dominion over the fish of the sea, over the birds of the air, and over every living thing that moves on the earth" (v. 28).

Fourth, the concepts of hierarchy and delegation have their roots in that perfect pre-Fall existence of man. For God, the ultimate CEO and founder of the universe, now delegates to man the responsibility to oversee the entire creation, including both plant and animal life. This should come as no surprise, since all of Scripture reflects God's orderly character.

The Hebrew word translated "formed" in Genesis 2:7, when God formed man from the dust of the ground, is *yasar*. It describes "the work of an artist, like a potter shaping an earthen vessel from clay."[2] Reflect if you will on this incredible work of God. Think about the parallel between God's creativity in fashioning man—the hairs on his head, the shape of arms and legs, the structure of muscle and skeleton, the texture and resilience of skin—and human creativity down through the centuries. In a sense, the work of every artist, every creative act done by any and every human being, in some way reflects that incredible creativity demonstrated by God when He fashioned our first parent. Without question, work at its origin was absolutely good.

After fashioning man from the dust of the ground—a work without human parallel—and breathing into his nostrils the breath of life, God carried out a third kind of work. He planted a garden. Here He delegated to man a new task—to maintain the garden as his residence.

We do the same today. As I write these words, spring has finally returned to Nebraska. It's May, and flowers are beginning to blossom. Our trees are in full bloom, and our grass, watered by drenching rains, is growing so fast we can hardly keep it cut. Many of our friends are planting tomatoes, cucumbers, bell peppers. My father-in-law, who lives in Louisiana, is well into his annual gardening process. Before summer is over, we will be eating the fruit of his labors.

And here in Genesis 2, I read of the Lord God planting a garden. The language of the text is amazing. Clearly God could have simply spoken this garden into existence. Yet Moses clearly wrote that He planted a garden eastward in Eden and placed man there. God worked to create the garden, man would work to maintain it (until sin entered and Adam and his wife would be cast out). As the narrative tells us, "The Lord God took the man and put him in the Garden of Eden to tend and keep it" (Genesis 2:15). Man had a specific place.

His place was in the garden, and his specific job or service was the ongoing responsibility to tend and care for it.

It is interesting that the very first use of the word *command* in the Bible has to do with caring for the garden and receiving sustenance from work. Clearly the framework for the concept of work as we understand it today is established here. God is the boss, Eden the workplace. Tending the garden and exercising dominion over creation constituted Adam's job duties. His compensation and benefits, as well as his limitations, were also spelled out. We might even call God's instructions to Adam the first job description.

Fifth, there is dignity and value in filling the role of a helper, a servant, or an assistant. "I will make him a helper comparable to him" (v. 18), God declares, and He begins to shape the first woman. Though many people consider the term "helper" to be demeaning, the term is actually used by the psalmist of the Lord God. "Our soul waits for the Lord; He is our *help* and our shield" (Psalm 33:20, emphasis added). Not only was a marriage established in Eden, there was also an interdependent working relationship.

Next, the Lord demonstrated that a partnership existed between Himself and Adam as co-laborers, even though God was clearly sovereign and in charge. God did what He alone was capable of doing, as He formed every beast of the field and every bird of the air (v. 19). Then He brought them to Adam to see what he would call them, and whatever Adam called each creature became its name.

SEEDBED FOR WORK

These pre-Fall chapters of Genesis provide us with a seed plot in which all the important concepts and implications for work today are rooted:

1. Work is an important part of the total picture of life for Christians. We often emphasize the priority of family, yet work chronologically preceded the establishment of the

home. God laid out Adam's job responsibility before He gave the man a mate. This is not to minimize family at all; yet it clearly demonstrates the need to maintain a comprehensive perspective on life, one that incorporates personal, family, work, worship, and community issues.

2. The spiritual dimension and our work are clearly linked. There is no sacred/secular distinction. Just as God was closely involved with Adam as both immediate supervisor and ultimate CEO, so He wants to be involved in our work. That's why the apostle Paul points out that Christians "serve the Lord Christ" (Colossians 3:24).

3. Work is an important aspect of both our calling from God and our personal identity. Before the Fall, God entrusted Adam with the responsibility to both till the ground—what may seem to us a relatively meaningless routine—and have dominion over all creation. This was his calling and his identity. His intrinsic purpose was to reflect God's glory, since he was made in God's image. The outworking of this was his exercising creativity and overseeing the garden God had made and in naming and overseeing the animal creation. Sometimes we like to caution people against finding their identity in their work. I agree that for the Christian our ultimate identity is wrapped up in the Person of Christ. Yet there is a sense in which, for both men and women, there is a degree of identity based on what we do.

4. Work is designed to provide meaning, order, and structure as well as provision for life. God gave Adam a job and used that job as a way of meeting his temporal needs. I believe this shows that God wants our work to have meaning.

5. God wants our work to demonstrate His moral and ethical standards. The apostle Paul called for thieves to change their occupation (see Ephesians 4:28) and to do so in order to be able to give. Clearly God intends for our work to enable us to meet our own needs and to allow us to engage in meaningful, loving service to others.

WHY DO WE WORK?

During our discussion, I asked members of the group why they worked. The conversation quickly turned lively.

"Just to bring home a paycheck," Cindy asserted. "Survival is the big issue."

Rich, the mechanic, nodded agreement. "I don't see how you can consider replacing somebody's water pump or working on an automatic transmission a ministry."

Deena, the psychologist, interjected her strong disagreement. "I think there is meaning in work. I've been reading psychologist Abraham Maslow, and he looks at our work from the standpoint of what he calls a hierarchy of need. At the bottom there's the need to earn money for food, shelter, protection, things like that. The next level involves social needs: acceptance, friendship, belonging. Then there's self-esteem and worth. At the top of the hierarchy he places our need for challenge, distinction, and fulfillment."

"But, Deena, that's the view of a secular psychologist," Art countered. "I don't think you can defend that from Scripture."

Art's question prompted me to continue our biblical study of work. "Let's look at Scripture," I told the group.

After recapping God's work in the first two chapters of Genesis, I suggested that the New Testament verifies Jesus' participation in creation. Then I mentioned the common Greek word for work in the New Testament. That word, *ergos,* means "work, deed, or business, a service or guide." It suggests that believers work so that they may perform acts of service and kindness. Such works are performed to help others in the name of Christ, including presenting the gospel. Dorcas, for example, was said to be full of "good works" (Acts 9:36). Barnabas and Paul were separated for missionary work, to which they were called (13:2) and which they completed and reported on once they had finished it (14:26). One of Paul's strongest desires was that he and those to whom he ministered would continually abound in "the work of the Lord" (1 Corinthians 15:58). As he told the Ephesians, "we were created in Christ Jesus unto good works" (Ephesians 2:10), including the work of the ministry (4:12).

However, Paul's interest was not limited to those whose work was in a vocational ministry. He wanted to see every believer established and fruitful in every good word and work (Colossians 1:10; 2 Thessalonians 2:17). He urged church leaders, both male and female, to demonstrate good works (1 Timothy 3:1; 5:10; Titus 2:7).

Now, not every one of these passages just cited refers to vocational employment. But they do show the intrinsic value placed on good works, both in the workplace and in life.

ULTIMATE MANDATES

On several occasions Jesus was asked what He considered to be the greatest commandment. His response was to point to Deuteronomy 6:4 and Leviticus 19:18, explaining that we are to love the Lord with all our heart and our neighbor as ourselves (Mark 12:29–31). I believe everything God expects of us can be summarized in these mandates to love God wholeheartedly and to love people unconditionally.

So how does work fit into these two ultimate mandates? A key purpose of work is to provide an opportunity to demonstrate loving service to God. Just as Adam worked as a partner and fellow laborer with God as well as His employee, so we should view our work as a service to the Lord Christ.

As I talked with the members of my panel, I discovered that many of them already viewed their work in this way. Those who did had discovered a major purpose in their career: to honor God and His Son.

Several also recognized work as an opportunity to serve people. For Deena it was a natural extension of what she does. "As a counselor, I'm there for hurting people. My goal is to meet their needs. In the process I want to point them to the Lord, who can ultimately meet all their needs. That's why

I counsel people from a Christian perspective." For Deena, counseling had become a way to love her neighbors as herself.

Vern looked at his business in the same way. "My companies employ several hundred people from all walks of life. I try to stress to our management people the importance of operating on principles of servant leadership. We are here to serve people, to help meet the needs of our clients. Our businesses are varied, but we seek to run them on biblical principles like the Golden Rule, which I believe expresses how we can love our neighbors as ourselves."

"I guess I'm really in the service business too," Cindy, the waitress, conceded. "In fact, since I came to see how serving people can also be a way to serve God, I've been able to avoid feeling cynical and burned out about my work. I still struggle with it—there are times I'd like to pour coffee all over some of my customers! But I'm getting there."

Out of these great commandments grows another legitimate aspect of work—fulfilling our own needs. Although the Bible doesn't command us to love ourselves, the phrase "love your neighbor as yourself" implies a legitimate self-interest. Work is one of the God-given means by which we take care of our own lives, providing both nourishment and personal value.

No, work is not a consequence of the Fall. It actually provides us with the opportunity to demonstrate wholehearted love to God and unconditional love for people, plus meet our own legitimate needs. From Paul's perspective, to "work in quietness and eat your own food" was the way to do good (2 Thessalonians 3:12–13). As Paul wrote to Timothy, it's un-Christian, even pagan, not to work to provide for the needs of your own family (1 Timothy 5:8).

In addition to providing for our families, work enables us to share with those who are in need. That seemed to be Paul's point when he called on those who previously earned their living dishonestly to enter some form of good, honest labor (Ephesians 4:28). To some degree Paul's principle may have been based on a lesson identified by King David about how God provides for our needs, enables us to give, and even helps us leave a legacy. In Psalm 37 David wrote, "I have been young and now I am old, yet I have not seen the righteous forsaken, nor his descendants begging bread. All day long he is gracious and lends, and his descendants are a blessing" (vv. 25–26 NASB). Through the years the poet king had learned he could trust God to provide basic needs as he worked hard and practiced generosity. That's a lesson that needs to be passed along from generation to generation.

As I talked with Vern about his business, I saw his perspective—how he was cooperating with God and people in his work. "We have a real estate investment firm. We'll take a piece of raw land; our planning division puts together a plan. Then our construction people go in, build a shopping center, apartments, maybe a restaurant, that provide income for people or other businesses that lease what we build. I make a good return on my investment, the businesses do well, and the employees earn a living. People benefit all up and down the line, and I think God is pleased with that."

"I think being a good mechanic can also please God," Rich added. "I may not be involved in any big business deals, but I know firsthand how frustrating it is to have a car that doesn't work right. If I do a good job, I not only earn a good living for my family, I also help my customers get to work in their cars. I'm helping my business, and even indirectly helping Vern's, since I work for a dealership that leases buildings and land from Vern's company."

One way we can reduce stress on the job is by seeing our jobs as a way to honor God by serving people, providing for our family's and our own needs, and then giving the credit to God. This perspective leads to greater contentment in our work and reduces the level of stress we feel in the workplace.

CHOOSING A VOCATION

Another way we can reduce stress in the workplace is to choose the right job for ourselves. So how do I decide which job I should do? After all, if work has value to God, it seems I should do the work that has the most value to God. Does the Bible say anything about picking the right line of work? No, but the above Bible passages certainly give us some important pointers concerning any job.

First, let's remember that no honest work is demeaning or lacking in opportunity to glorify God. Any job, no matter how menial or common it may seem, has value. Paul pointed this out when he wrote to the Colossian church to urge those who were slaves to obey their masters with "sincerity of heart, fearing God. And whatever you do, do your work heartily as to the Lord and not for men . . . for you serve the Lord Christ" (Colossians 3:22–24). What a crucial principle. Menial, daily work is ultimately a ministry to the Lord Jesus Christ! So when Cindy waits tables or Rich works as a mechanic, there is value to God in the tasks they perform. It's an important perspective for us to take with us to our work today.

Second, Paul urged masters and slaves alike to exercise justice and fairness—masters in their rule, slaves in their work (Colossians 4:1; Ephesians 6:8–9). Today's employers and employees should follow the same principles. Employees should obey with authentic respect and a sincere, honest heart, just as if they worked for Christ Himself. Paul used the principle of sowing and reaping to reinforce God's promise to take care of those who do well in their work (v. 8). Furthermore, those who employ others (in Paul's day, the masters) were to give up the use of threats and to serve their employees honestly, compassionately, and from the heart (v. 9). Both here in Ephesians and throughout the New Testament, Paul emphasized our need to make God and people our priority, an emphasis consistent with Christ's demand that we love God wholeheartedly and people unconditionally.

WORK IN BALANCE

From Paul's approach we see the importance of balance, putting work in its rightful place. Work is not to be elevated to the point of workaholism, nor should it be minimized to a "secular and unimportant" level. Some practical implications come to mind from these observations.

First, make sure your work gets your wholehearted devotion when you are working, but don't let it creep into other areas of your life. Missionary and martyr Jim Elliot once said, "Wherever you are be all there. Live to the hilt each day what you believe to be the will of God."[3] I think that includes focusing on work when you're working, avoiding daydreaming and distractions so that you'll be able to bring closure to each day's work without having to "take it home with you."

Second, make sure you are not giving too much attention or emotional energy to your work when you're home with family. I've known individuals who were careful not to spend too many hours at the office but who didn't mind spending hour after hour going over reports at home or discussing business plans with an associate on the phone—often with wives and children getting the message that "we're not nearly as important as work."

Third, cultivate the Sabbath rest, that time of relaxation and refreshment. This rest and renewal includes both weekend time and proper use of your vacation periods. Follow the exhortation of Christ, who invited the disciples to "come apart and rest awhile," before He led them back into the intense, important labor He had entrusted to them. Take your vacations and use them to relax, not to work on upcoming projects and not just to do maintenance projects at home. Painting the house may be OK during part of a one-week vacation, but don't expend your entire vacation time on home improvements.

Finally, remember that in every area of life, ultimate accountability goes directly back to the Lord Himself. Do your work as though the Lord was right there with you in the shop, on the job, in the field, at the hospital, or wherever you work. After all, He is.

CHAPTER FIVE

BACK TO THE FALL: WHERE BAD STRESS BEGAN

S ometime during the wee morning hours, perhaps about 3:00 A.M., you awoke from a sound sleep, went to the bathroom, and then crawled back into bed. But you just couldn't drop off to sleep again. Maybe you were thinking about that meeting with your boss or the report you hadn't completed or the computer program that was giving you fits. Finally, at about 5:00 A.M. you fell asleep.

Now, as you finally awake, instead of seeing early daylight, bright sunshine is streaming through your bedroom blinds. The alarm clock announces what you feared: 8:05 A.M. And you're supposed to be at work by 8:30!

You throw on the coffee pot, rush to the shower where you nearly slip on a half-used bar of soap, cut yourself shaving (or jab mascara in your eye), burn your tongue on the hot coffee, then spill part of it on your tie (or blouse).

As usual the freeway is clogged—you hoped it would have cleared by this late hour. You arrive at work and try vainly to tiptoe past the receptionist's desk; she hands you two pink call slips and a folder from the boss.

You head for your desk, knowing how much has piled up in your "in" box. The door to your office is open; you see the boss standing just inside—and he isn't smiling. *How can anybody consider a job good?* you wonder. It's so stressful.

STRESS RESPONSE

Although the effects of stress may be bad, stress itself is actually neutral. In fact, stress is so common every single one of us faces it. Years ago Hans Selye, one of the pioneers of medicine, introduced what was then considered a revolutionary concept: every worker, no matter his or her job, is subject to stress. In his landmark book *The Stress of Life,* Selye pointed out, "The beggar who suffers from hunger and the glutton who overeats, the little shopkeeper with his constant fears of bankruptcy and the rich merchant struggling for yet another million: they are all under stress."[1]

Selye defined stress as the nonspecific response of the body to any demand. He called this the general adaptation syndrome. However, he did not consider stress to be bad or something to always be avoided.[2]

How can that be? Certain stresses, such as those experienced during creativity, successful work, and exhilaration, can be beneficial. Consider this chapter's opening stressful scenario. The sound of an alarm clock can be stressful; yet without it, many of us would never get up or make it to work on time. Even while you are asleep your heart continues to beat, your lungs breathe—even your brain is at work as you dream. Selye wrote, "Stress can only be avoided by dying."[3]

Selye argued that the notion of someone's being "under stress" is wrong. He considered that statement just as meaningless as pointing out that someone is "running a temperature." Everyone runs a temperature, hopefully 98.6 degrees; similarly, everyone has a degree of stress. What we actually should say is, "He is under an excess of stress," or, "His temperature is above normal."

According to Selye, stress begins to cause problems when it produces a strong response. The normal release of hormones, such as adrenaline, enables our bodies to cope with a stressful situation. What Selye labeled the "stressor," the event, is the overabundant buildup of adrenaline in the bloodstream.[4] When this process, called "fight or flight," happens over and over, it can lead to physical illness. As noted earlier, as much as 70 percent of all medical disorders are stress-related. Such illnesses cost American businesses $150 billion each year. An estimated 30 million Americans now have major coronary problems; each year 1 million adults suffer heart attacks, and 8 million have ulcers—most of which are related to excess stress.[5] No wonder stress is often labeled a killer.

THE ORIGIN OF STRESS

Where did our stress get its start? How did it work its way into the workplace and begin causing the havoc we see today?

As we have seen, negative, or "bad," stress was not part of the original creation. Before he sinned, Adam fulfilled a meaningful existence doing the job God had given him. Responding to good stress, Adam named the animals, tilled the Garden of Eden, and worked without shame next to his wife and partner, Eve.

Then in Genesis 3, the first man and woman sinned, and the consequences were immediate and dramatic. Not surprisingly, the first and most immediate impact was on Adam's workplace.

Picture the scene. It's the cool of late afternoon. The Lord God Himself comes into the garden to visit with Adam. But the man and his wife have hidden themselves among the trees. The voice of the Lord calls out, "Adam, where are you?" This was not a request for information. God knew where Adam was, both physically and spiritually. It was a call for Adam to admit that tension had been created between his Maker and himself.

Adam's reply gave the first clue to the devastating consequences of his actions. "I heard Your voice in the garden, and I was afraid" (v. 10). It was the first negative emotion— fear—and one frequently associated with stress today. Think of the stressful elements in your workplace—conflicts with fellow workers, equipment failures, an overbearing boss. You'll probably find fear associated with each one, a fear that originated with Adam's fall into sin.

"I was naked," the man went on to say, "and I hid myself" (v. 10). People have been hiding ever since—refusing to communicate, failing to disclose, reluctant to let others see them as they really are, even engaging in outright deceit. All these have become sources of negative stress, and they extend to our places of work.

When God asked the inevitable confrontational question, the man blamed "the woman You gave me"; and she in turn tried to blame the serpent (vv. 12–13). Hiding, covering up, lying, blaming others, allowing conflicts to develop—that's how stress in the workplace began.

Notice the consequences God spelled out. First, there was the conflict between the serpent and the woman, then sorrow in conception and pain in childbearing, plus conflicts and power struggles between wife and husband (v. 16). Then, to paraphrase His warning in verses 17–19, God told Adam, "You listened to your wife instead of obeying Me. Now your workplace is cursed. Life will be filled with hard work. Obstacles like thorns and thistles will cause futile, frustrating activity. You will still be able to earn a living, but it will be infinitely harder. You'll do it in the sweat of your face, Adam. And ultimately it will take its toll, and you will suffer death."

I see a remarkable parallel between Selye's view of the stresses of life and the Bible's. Selye said we cannot escape stress. It is there. Furthermore, it ultimately leads to disease, even death. That's exactly what Moses recorded in Genesis. God's message to Adam and Eve when He confronted their sin was, "Now life will be filled with stress, and ultimately it will lead you to death."

It is an amazing cause-and-effect chain. Sin leads to negative stress, including stress in the workplace. Stress will ultimately lead to death.

 **STRESS TEST** ....

Stress on Your Job

Bad stress comes from an excessive level of physical and emotional pressures. Maybe you have or are feeling excess stress in several of the following areas. Check all the boxes that apply to your work setting. The more you check, the greater the level of stress at your job.

☐ *I perform a task that puts frequent strain on a body part (such as back or wrist).*

☐ *I sometimes feel that my job is meaningless and not worth my time.*

☐ *I perform a repetitive task that seems boring.*

☐ *From time to time a boss, co-worker, or I ignore ethics and violate rules through cheating, lying, or other deceitful practices.*

☐ *I feel irritated with one or more people at work.*

☐ *I have conflicts with one or more co-workers.*

....

THE NATURE OF SIN

Clearly, bad stress started in the Garden of Eden, with our fall into sin. Thus, to understand some of the causes of bad stress, we should ask ourselves, "Exactly what is sin?"

Missing the Mark

The clearest definition probably comes from Paul's carefully worded argument in Romans 3: "For all have sinned and fall short of the glory of God" (v. 23). The Greek word for sin, *harmatanō*, also expresses the major idea behind the Old Testament word for sin. The word has the idea of deviating from a course or missing a mark, primarily by falling short.

In the Old Testament book of Judges, the word is used in describing a squad of warriors from the tribe of Benjamin. All these men were talented left-handers. In fact, had they lived today, they might have all been drafted by a major league baseball team and signed to lucrative contracts, because they were men with outstanding throwing ability and control. Scripture recorded how they could hurl stones at a hairline target without missing (Judges 20:16). Interestingly, the Hebrew word translated "miss" here is elsewhere rendered "sin."

The lesson in terms of the nature of sin is obvious. These men could throw their stones without falling short of the mark. In contrast, sin is a failure to hit God's standard; it is falling short. That's exactly what Adam and Eve did when they ate the forbidden fruit. By disobeying God, they fell short of His perfection and brought about the moral pollution of the perfect stream that flowed through their workplace.

Disobedience

Not only does sin involve falling short, it is also an act of disobedience. In Genesis 2:16–17, God had clearly pointed out His expectations to Adam concerning the workplace. The man had been charged with dressing and keeping the garden and instructed not to eat of the Tree of the Knowledge of Good and Evil. Yet he clearly committed an act of disobedience. The same thing happened in the next generation when Abel presented an offering to God from the flock and Cain brought the fruit of the ground. The issue wasn't that vegetables were bad and animals were good. Nor was it that God considered Abel good and accepted his offering but judged Cain evil. The point is that one man obeyed; to use our terminology, he hit the mark. The other missed the mark by refusing to obey God. The issue was simple obedience. The disobedience of Cain in a sense reflects the effect of the pollution of sin from Cain's parents.

Total Pollution

To what degree has the stream of humanity been affected by sin? The effects are total, as we can see from Paul's simple statement that "all have sinned and fall short of the glory of God" (Romans 3:23). Later the apostle wrote, "Through one man sin entered the world, and death through sin, and thus death spread to all men, because all sinned" (Romans 5:12).

The implications for humanity are clear. Adam's sin injected sin into the stream of humanity. All of us have been polluted by its effects. Every one of us faces the ultimate consequence—death. We commit acts of sin. We inherit a sin nature from our parents, one they ultimately derived from Adam. We also have sin imputed to our accounts because of our participation in the race of which Adam is the head. And we are spiritually dead, separated from God.

There is a sense in which, although the story of Adam and Eve is historical, it is our story as well. Today children are born into the world, experience temptation, and fall into personal sin. We face the same kind of temptation that Eve was confronted with—the lust of the flesh confronts us, just as Eve saw that the tree was good for food. We are captivated by the "lust of the eyes," much as Eve was drawn to the pleasant appearance of the fruit. And as Satan the deceiver assured her that the tree would make her wise, so we respond to temptations related to the pride of life (1 John 2:16).

Think of the variety of words used in Scripture to talk about sin: evil, ungodliness, wickedness, lawlessness, error, unbelief, and many others. Ultimately our sin has caused us to become spiritually dead.

SIN AND WORK

So what is the direct connection between sin and workplace stress? It is of first importance to understand that work is not a punishment from God. Work itself is intrinsically good, not evil. The curse did not impose work as a punishment or consequence, nor did it remove the value of work. Centuries after Adam, when Lamech became the father of Noah, he predicted, "This one will comfort us concerning our work and the toil of our hands, because of the ground which the Lord has cursed" (Genesis 5:29). Noah's name meant "rest." It seems that God gave Noah's father insight that Noah would provide rest and protection and ultimately give meaning to the daily toil and rigor that had resulted from the curse.

However, work became more difficult because of sin's polluting effects. To understand how this works, let's go back to our analogy of a stream. When I was a child growing up near Birmingham, Alabama, I discovered a delightful spring in a cavelike depression in a hillside just a mile from our home. As the water flowed out of the ground, a little hollowed-out place had formed in the rock, just about the right size for dipping both hands for a cool, refreshing drink. That little spot at the headwaters of a creek provided a thirsty boy with many a delightful drink of water.

However, neither I nor my friends would drink from that same creek even a mile downstream. By that point, pollutants from the fields and from nearby steel mills and other industries had seeped into the water, making it undrinkable. There was even seepage from nearby septic tanks and sewage treatment facilities. What had once been an unpolluted stream was drastically and negatively affected by pollutants.

In the same way the gracious gift of God—work—was affected by man's disobedience. Remember, the value and purpose of work did not change. Even after the Fall, people still answered to God, worked for God, and served as co-workers with God. People still had the responsibility to till the ground. However, the phrase "the sweat of your face" underscored just how difficult work would become.

Yet even in the face of the difficulty of work, God promised Israel that it is "the Lord your God . . . who gives you power to get wealth" (Deuteronomy 8:18). God's ongoing provision of energy for work was to serve as a reminder to them—and us—to maintain an attitude of gratefulness.

Centuries later, Solomon offered an important perspective on his own work. The best of life, humanly speaking, came from the hand of God through His provision of good results from our labor, which He gives to be enjoyed (Ecclesiastes 2:24). Solomon went on to say, "I have seen the God-given task with which the sons of men are to be occupied. He has made everything beautiful in its time. . . . I know there is nothing better for them than to rejoice and to do good in their lives, and also that every man should eat and drink and enjoy the good of all his labor—it is the gift of God" (3:10–13).

Clearly, from Solomon's perspective, labor, even "under the sun," has great benefit. Work is God's gift, and through it He provides for basic needs such as food and drink. Tasks are to be carried out with joy and done well. Ultimately, work is a trust from God, both in its process and its product (Ecclesiastes 5:18–19). So, although the process has been stained by the effects of sin, work still has great value.

SIN'S DREADFUL IMPACT ON WORK

The First Harsh Impact of Sin: Bad Stress

Sin has made work much more difficult, primarily by introducing the element of bad stress. The first job I ever held was in a service station, working long hours for two dollars a day changing flat tires, washing cars, stocking the soft drink machine, and rushing out to the gasoline pumps to ask the question, "Fill 'er up? Premium or regular?" (There was no such thing as self-service back then.)

I considered my job to be very hard and the wages low, even for those days. At times I felt like quitting. But I didn't have to look far to find people who worked much harder than I. My boss, Mr. Haygood, also worked in the mines. I would arrive at the station at about 6:00 A.M. He would work there with me for the first half hour, getting me started for the day, then drive down Highway 78 toward the mines. Later that afternoon, usually between 4:00 and 4:30, he would arrive back at the station, covered with coal dust, sweat-soaked, and exhausted. From what he told me, very few jobs were more stressful than that of a coal miner.

My own father started off shoveling coal as a fireman on a steam engine on the Southern Railway. The work was hot, nasty, and sometimes dangerous. In fact, when I was a young child, Dad was laid up for several months with a broken leg as a result of a collision between two steam locomotives. The hours were usually long, the work sometimes boring. But Dad loved it, and he gave it all he had.

My grandfather and several of my uncles worked in a different field of employment. Their stresses were more mental than physical. They sold life insurance, which in those days meant "walking a debit" to collect premiums. As one of my uncles put it, you never knew whether you would be able to collect what you were after or whether someone would come out and give you the third degree, or maybe even threaten you with physical harm.

Without question, sin has made work more difficult. Today, although more offices are air conditioned and many chairs and desks have been redesigned to lessen back strain and wrist fatigue, we still have to perform tasks that may be repetitive, relate to people who are difficult to work with, and put up with the day-to-day effects of stress.

The Second Harsh Impact of Sin: Our Relationships

Consider all the people you work with. Try to think about one who isn't a sinner or whose old nature you haven't glimpsed from time to time. That's why we have conflicts at work. It explains why Adam and Eve began experiencing conflict and why Cain ultimately killed Abel. The Fall has drastically affected our relationships at work. Partners who have been close to each other for years separate in an outburst of conflict. Men and women angrily turn in their resignations from good jobs.

The Third Harsh Impact of Sin: Moral Standards

Perhaps the place where we most clearly see the effect of the Fall is in the area of ethics and moral standards. The Whitewater scandal threatened President Clinton's administration, yet allegations of misdeeds by previous presidents have also rocked the White House. Companies that have collapsed under the weight of fraudulent stock transactions or wrongfully engineered mergers have cost many employees their jobs.

The moral low road affects individual workers as well. Some obtain their jobs by lying on résumés; others cheat on their taxes. White-collar crimes by workers and managers cost businesses as much as $40 billion a year.[6] Individuals are ripped off by companies, and employees are taken advantage of by uncaring bosses. Employees steal from companies, justifying their actions by saying, "Life isn't fair anyway."

Finally, there is a sense in which all of us, to one degree or another, are affected by indirect participation in evil and its effects. We pay taxes to a government that may engage in wrong actions. We purchase our groceries in a store owned by a conglomerate that also owns gambling casinos, or we purchase products made by a company that manufactures abortion-inducing substances.

All of this creates stress as we attempt to do what is right in an evil-plagued workplace. To the degree that we can, we should take steps to avoid direct participation in or support of evil. But none of us can completely escape the corruption and pollution we find in our world. As Jesus said of His disciples, we are in the world but not of it. And He didn't pray that we would be taken out of the world, but that we would be preserved and sanctified from the evil.

This brings us to the ultimate effect of sin on the workplace: the sinfulness in our own hearts and, in one sense, our own attitudes taken to the workplace make a major contribution to stress. I remember talking with Mickey, a rugged construction worker. Mickey didn't mind working hard under the right circumstances—for example, when he went deer hunting or helped on a project at church. Yet, when it came to his job, he told me on more than one occasion, "I'm not going to let them get the whole eight hours out of me. They have to work hard to get whatever they get." It didn't take a rocket scientist to figure out what Mickey meant. He worked only as hard as he had to. Working heartily as to the Lord just wasn't part of his concept of employment.

Each Christian faces a similar conflict each day. We can go to our jobs committed to working heartily as to the Lord and serving people, or we can carry our own selfish ambition, our laziness, and our desire to manipulate and control people to work—and add to the stresses of our workplace.

Perhaps an attitude check is in order. Is our approach at work to step on others as we strive to climb the ladder of success? Is our primary motivation money and all we can obtain with it? Is it our desire to do as little as possible to keep our job and continue to collect our paycheck? Or do we use work as an escape from pressures and problems at home or unresolved issues from the past, perhaps even to prove to an abusive parent just how successful we can be? Regular evaluation and housecleaning of our attitudes can help us not only to survive but even to thrive in the rat race of the workplace.

The Fourth Harsh Impact of Sin: Futility

Sin has added one more negative to our work. Much of what we do seems futile or pointless. Earlier we considered Solomon's "under the sun" perspective from Ecclesiastes. One of the key words Solomon used throughout the book, *hebel,* describes the futile, fleeting, and temporal nature of life. A sense of futility is a major component of the curse, and according to the apostle Paul it touches virtually every aspect of creation (Romans 8:20).

This is an important perspective to have as we consider the connection between work and stress. Raymond, a talented young man, told me that his job was boring and repetitive. Amazingly, Raymond was involved in a Christian ministry, helping produce materials designed to lead unsaved people to personal faith in Christ and to build up believers in their faith. The tasks Raymond performed, though somewhat repetitive in nature, contributed directly to putting those materials into a form in which people could grasp and understand important, life-changing spiritual truths. Yet, for Raymond, work had become futile and frustrating.

As Raymond and I discussed his frustrations, we looked at Solomon's statements in Ecclesiastes and Paul's observation in Romans 8. Raymond began to understand that futility would never fully disappear from the workplace. He began to gain a sense of meaning in his work, seeing the spiritual impact of the materials he prepared.

I have come to this viewpoint personally in my own ministry. I have invested many hours preparing messages, studying Scripture for writing and radio, and seeing to technical details. There are aspects of my work that can be exciting, challenging, and thrilling; yet much of the preparation is what might be called "grunt work."

At a conference where I was speaking recently, a man lamented the drudgery and routine of his job. "I'd love to do something like you do in radio," he said. "Or maybe preach like Chuck Swindoll or teach the Bible like Woodrow Kroll." I countered by asking, "How much drudgery time do you suppose Dr. Kroll or Chuck Swindoll put into their preparations?" His reply indicated that he had no idea that any drudgery might be involved. Yet teaching and preaching God's Word consists of about 90 percent perspiration and only 10 percent inspiration. Digging to find out what God's Word means and coming up with just the right illustration to help people understand and apply it to their situations can be tedious.

The same thing is true for the insurance agent faced with mountains of paperwork, the counselor who has to write up and document each case, and the airline pilot who must keep up with the latest technical innovations and handle all the logging for each flight. Even in the production of radio ministries there is a great deal of attention to detail, some of it routine and boring.

OUR RESPONSE

Knowing how sin contributes to workplace stress, we need to respond to others with love and forgiveness, as well as recognize our own shortcomings. Of course, not all job-related stress is the result of our own individual sins. Some of it comes from the Fall, a sort of fallout from the choice of Adam and Eve. Yet all too frequently our personal failures and capacity for sin contribute to the problem. We can and should deal with our own sinful responses.

Shereen works for a Christian organization that provides an important service for people from all walks of life. She finds great fulfillment in her vocation. Her job involves public relations and advertising, and she does it well. Yet she works for a boss who is extremely hard-driving. He often ridicules her in front of others, criticizes her work unfairly, and seems to expect more of her than he does her colleagues.

Her responsibility in such a situation is to "speak the truth in love" (Ephesians 4:15), to confront what is out of order and inappropriate. She could ask for a private meeting with her boss, or even go to the human resources department at her company. Instead, she chooses to "stew in her juices," allowing bitterness and anger to build up. She considers her work very stressful, and she frequently goes home with a headache that hinders her from relating to her family. She gets angry at her children over relatively inconsequential things and even experiences physical symptoms. In addition, she finds herself carrying out a form of passive rebellion at work, slowing down projects, sometimes even doing the opposite of what her boss wants done.

Shereen knows what Scripture says about not holding grudges and about confronting with love. She's just not acting on them. Like many of us, she has failed to apply the principle Jesus explained: "If you know these things, happy are you if you do them" (John 13:17).

Life offers each of us a series of decision points, opportunities to choose. Our choices will determine the effectiveness of our lives and work. How will you respond to stress points, such as pressing deadlines, expectations of your boss or fellow workers, and your own expectations, fundamental needs, and personal wants? As management authority Stephen Covey points out, "With all these factors acting on us, it is important to remember that a moment of choice is just that—a moment of choice."[7] According to Covey and others who have analyzed the nature of such choices, we have several possible responses. We can simply react automatically, without thinking. We can allow circumstances or people to control us. Or we can step back, evaluate on the basis of our convictions, then use our abilities to make conscience-directed decisions. The choice is ours.

Very few of us would consider our work to be equivalent to life in a concentration camp. Yet psychiatrist Victor Frankl pointed out that even in Nazi concentration camps there were those whose lives offered "sufficient proof that everything can be taken from a man but one thing: the last of the human freedoms—to choose one's attitude in any given set of circumstances, to choose one's own way."[8]

For those who, like Frankl, were incarcerated in concentration camps and for those of us today who feel chained to a desk or sentenced to an unbearable job, there are still choices to make daily, even hourly. Sure, other people or mitigating circumstances may be involved. But ultimately we hold the responsibility to choose to do what is right. Some choices may seem inconsequential—not to steal paper clips or office supplies, not to come in late and leave early, not to gossip about a fellow worker, spread an ugly rumor, or allow a negative attitude to fester.

Our choices lead to practices that become habits, affecting our attitudes and lives. So it is important not to bow to the tyranny of the urgent, the social expectations of others, the negative influence of our past, or even the desire to avoid pain or push our own personal agenda. Instead, we should base our choices on those deep-seated values we get from our faith, the values we find in Scripture of humble and cheerful service. How do we establish those deep-seated values? To a significant degree, almost every choice we make will reflect the two key principles we discussed earlier:

Loving God with all your heart

Loving your neighbor as you love yourself

Jesus made clear that these two imperatives provided the foundation for the entire biblical revelation of His day. Today we face choices on the job and in life that seem far too complex to be governed by such simple principles. Yet in our quest for complexity we often overlook those two love principles that can make the difference between our "hitting the target" or "missing the mark."

RESOURCES FOR CHOOSING

Some time ago the one-hundred-ton American space shuttle Atlantis blasted into orbit and was steered to a successful rendezvous with the Russian space station Mir. With these two massive spacecraft hurtling through space at more than 17,000 miles an hour, the margin for error was incredibly narrow. Yet, with the help of his computer navigational system, the power of his rocket engines, and the assistance of a team of colleagues at Houston's Mission Control, shuttle pilot Charles Pecourt was able to link up the two huge space vehicles.

Each Christian has within him or her a far more effective internal power supply than any rocket system: the Holy Spirit. We also have access to the most perfect and complete source of guidance for every situation: the Word of God. Plus, we can benefit from the collective wisdom and support of others in the body of Christ, the church. These resources will not remove all the stress from our work or our lives. But they can help us successfully navigate the myriad decisions we face every day, providing us with the resources in each moment of choice to select the course of action that best reflects those two fundamental mandates—loving Him and loving people.

Sure, it's stressful for a Christian to work in a foundry, a mall, or a large office. But if I am committed to loving God with all my heart, I will be able to reduce my stress by choosing to do whatever demonstrates my love for Him. Furthermore, my choices in relationships, even with that impossible colleague or that hard-to-get-along-with boss, will lead to communication styles and attitudes that are governed by the "love your neighbor as yourself" principle.

PART TWO

THE CAUSES OF STRESS IN THE WORKPLACE

CHAPTER SIX

PRESSURES AND PERCEPTIONS

On the coldest Monday morning of a Nebraska winter, as temperatures hovered in the single digits and wind chills approached minus ten degrees, two workers went out to start their cars. Both discovered they had dead batteries.

Billy had parked his car in the garage the night before. He was shocked that his battery was bad, since he had replaced it the previous year. His car was five years old, but he tried to keep it in tip-top shape. Susie hadn't been able to park her car indoors. Although she drove a late-model sedan, she had found it difficult to start her car on several occasions.

When their batteries failed that chilly Monday morning, Billy and Susie felt the stress build. Both had responsibilities to take care of at work. Both needed to be on time. And both faced the strong likelihood that they wouldn't be on time. In fact, they realized they could be anywhere from several minutes to more than an hour late.

Not only did Susie and Billy feel stressed, both experienced the physiologic reaction sometimes referred to as the "stress response." Both felt anxious. Their heart rate accelerated and their blood pressure climbed. In spite of the cold, both broke out in sweat. Billy pounded his fists on the steering wheel, and Susie muttered "Why me? I didn't need this!"

COGNITIVE APPRAISAL

Billy and Susie both began to mentally appraise or evaluate the situation, performing what most stress experts call "cognitive appraisal." Such appraisals are usually the key factor in how we handle stress. Let's take a brief look at the cognitive appraisals of Billy and Susie in order to understand and learn from their responses.

The first thing Billy did was tell himself

This is so stupid of me. I should have known my battery would likely fail on a Monday. Why didn't I have it checked over the weekend when I gassed up my car? Sure, I remembered to check my oil—even had them put air in that right front tire that has a slow leak. But I didn't even think about the battery. How dumb of me!

And my boss is expecting my report this morning. The only way I can have it ready is to get to work early. Now I can't even get there on time. My boss will consider me irresponsible—after all, a couple of years ago I was a day late getting a report in. My boss has pretty stringent standards. I might even be fired. I can just see him now, waiting there, with all the other employees aware that he is about to lower the boom, give me the ax, hand me a pink slip. It will be the most humiliating and shameful thing in my entire life. What a disaster! I'm just an absolute failure. I can't succeed at work. Worse, I can't even keep track of my car.

As you might suspect, Billy's chain of thoughts left him incredibly "stressed out." This pattern of thinking would leave him unable to function at anywhere near an efficient level, even when he does arrive at work. Contrast Susie's thought processes.

Boy, I wish this hadn't happened. I don't know why these things always seem to occur on Monday. It's like there's a gremlin somewhere gumming up the works. I probably should have had that battery checked, especially when I noticed the car was a little hard to start last week when it was snowing. But then, I've never been very good with cars. I wish I was better at keeping up with things like that, but I'm not.

I wonder how my boss will feel when I apologize to her? I know she was expecting me to be early today. She won't have my report on her desk first thing this morning, and I still need to give it a "once over" on the word processor before I hand it in. Oh well, she has probably had flat tires or dead batteries too.

This is not my favorite way to start the workweek, but at least I'm not stranded by the side of the road. I did renew my AAA membership, and they promised the truck would be here to give me a jump-start in less than an hour. I heard about a three-car pileup on the freeway on the last traffic report. At least I wasn't involved in something like that. Sure, this is one of those roadblocks on the highway of life, but I can think of a lot worse things that could have happened.

Both Billy and Susie wound up a half hour late to work on the particular Monday in question. Can you guess which one had a really lousy rest of the day and which one was able to bounce back relatively quickly? Yes, Susie managed to get a grip on her stress and dealt well with the rest of the stresses of her workday. Billy, on the other hand, never seemed able to bounce back. Things were out of sync all day, and before the day was out, he actually felt physically ill.

MENTAL STRESS

Billy and Susie illustrate an important lesson about stress. It's more than just what happens to you, or even how your body responds. One of the key causes of stress involves how we perceive the events that cause stress.

In chapter 1 counselor Chris Thurman mentioned how our cognitive perceptions can ease or intensify stress (see subhead "Mind and Body"). During our lunch together, Chris also mentioned "Hooks' Law." It goes something like this: Material under stress will return to its original condition if the strain produced by stress falls within the "elastic limit" of the material. If the strain exceeds the elastic limit, permanent damage to the material will result. The key is that the object is able to flex to a certain point.

Similarly, we must flex, or adjust, as stress intensifies. The stressor is the event that brings wear and tear on our body or mind, according to Hans Selye. Those events can range from an equipment failure that brings the assembly line to a halt to sarcastic comments from an overbearing boss (who, unknown to us, has just been chewed out by his boss for failing to make quota and who may have also experienced a major run-in with his wife the night before). What matters most is not the event but how we respond to it.

STRESSED-OUT APOSTLE

In the New Testament the apostle Paul experienced such a time of stress. His original vocation as tentmaker was probably a fairly low-stress occupation. But when he became an apostle, traveling the world to represent Jesus Christ, he exposed himself to incredible stressors—things like angry mobs, shipwrecks, hard work, going without food, spending time in jail, even being beaten for his faith.

Writing to the church in Corinth—a source of more than a little of Paul's vocational stress—he told about the stress he had faced in his service to God. In 2 Corinthians 6:4–7 Paul listed ten different forms of stress, followed by eight specific inner qualities that helped him cope with pressure.

Earlier in 2 Corinthians, the apostle had talked about a specific kind of adversity he experienced in Asia Minor, a sit-

 **STRESS TEST**

Ten Tough Jobs

The apostle Paul found pressures even in the relatively low-stress occupation of tentmaker. Today all jobs bring stress, though some seem to carry an extra amount of industrial-strength stress. The National Institute on Worker's Compensation (NIWC) has identified some of the toughest jobs stresswise in America. Can you guess what the top five stress-inducing jobs are? Write them down on a sheet of paper. Then look at the top ten, shown below, as determined by the NIWC.

1. *inner-city high school teacher*
2. *police officer*
3. *miner*
4. *air traffic controller*
5. *medical intern*
6. *stockbroker*
7. *journalist*
8. *customer service complaint department worker*
9. *waitress*
10. *secretary*

Source: *Newsweek*, 25 April 1988, 40.

uation that went beyond anything he could handle in his own strength—in fact, it caused him to despair of even life itself (1:8–9). This particular stressful event, not specifically identified by the apostle, was considered by him to be a virtual "sentence of death." Yet his response was not to allow it to cause him to despair. Instead, Paul chose to turn from relying on his own ability to trusting in the God who had raised Jesus from the dead. It also drove him to depend on his friends in

Corinth both for prayer support and for personal encouragement through a gift they sent (v. 11).

Later Paul described his stresses in detail. There were troubles or pressures, hardships or difficulties, and a variety of distresses or "tight spots." He listed three specific kinds of adversity—beatings, imprisonments, and riots—which he had experienced during a visit to Philippi (Acts 16:19–23). His calling had led to hard work, sleepless nights, and hunger (2 Corinthians 6:4–5). Yet the apostle sought to cope by means of eight specific inner qualities: (1) purity, (2) godly knowledge, (3) steadfastness, (4) kindness toward people, (5) the power of the Holy Spirit, (6) sincere love, (7) God's protection from evil, and (8) the armor of righteous living.

Adjusting our perspective when stresses hit is a key step in handling them effectively. Because of the above eight qualities, the apostle Paul dealt successfully with the paradoxes of his work. At times he was honored and at other times dishonored, sometimes spoken evil of and at other times good, sometimes branded as a deceiver and at other times accepted as true. Sometimes he felt unknown and unappreciated, while at other times he was accepted and affirmed. Sometimes he was exposed to danger of death itself, but he often experienced the joy of life. At times he was destitute, though at other times he had enough to be able to share with others. On occasion he faced great sorrow, yet he always experienced God's joy (vv. 8–10). Paul's open candor in sharing these stresses gives us some idea of the fact that stressors are real and can affect our physical and emotional health.

ESCAPE IMPOSSIBLE

One solution to stress we've probably all fantasized about is somehow being able to escape stress entirely. We may envision getting away—perhaps permanently—to the mountains, the beach, or some idyllic spot totally free of stress, where we will never suffer interruptions, experience adversity, or encounter dead batteries. Don't hold your breath, friend.

Several years ago we were invited to present a seminar in the U.S. Virgin Islands, one of the most beautiful and idyllic vacation spots in the world. The seminar was to take place in June, but we needed to nail down the arrangements, so the organization we were working with offered to fly Kathy and me to the Virgin Islands for a weekend to scout out the area, determine what preparations needed to be made, and make sure everything was lined up for the June conference. It was a nasty job but somebody had to do it.

When we landed on Saint Thomas, the largest of the U.S. Virgin Islands, we were met by a young man named Peter, who worked for the local Christian radio station. He had arranged to have a friend give us a helicopter tour of the island—a thoroughly enjoyable experience—then take us to one of the most beautiful resort hotels on the island. During the weekend we swam in both the Caribbean and the Atlantic, snorkeled in Trunk Bay—labeled as one of the ten most beautiful beaches in the world—hiked, bicycled, sailed, and ate delicious seafood. We took care of the conference arrangements in record time, then devoted most of our stay to enjoying one of the world's ultimate vacation spots.

Kathy and I might have gained the impression that this natural paradise was somehow free of life's common stresses. However, in talking to individuals there, and during our conference a few months later, we learned that life could be just as stressful in the Virgin Islands as in Texas, Nebraska, Missouri, or Louisiana.

In fact, even if you are employed as a ski-lift operator in a mountain resort or a crew member on a charter cruise boat, you will still have stress. No workplace is stress free. Although there will be times away, times for a break—and there should be—stresses will continue to affect us all. The question is, How will we respond to that stress?

Furthermore, we may not always be aware of being under stress. We may have fooled ourselves into thinking that we are not under stress when we actually are. Stress affects high-pressure lives, but it can also affect those whose lives seem relatively pressure free. You don't have to be an executive dashing through a busy airport to catch a plane to feel the effects of stress. In fact, I have talked with several individuals who reached the "golden years of retirement," yet who felt incredibly stressed because of an uncertainty about their retirement income or whether Social Security and Medicare would continue to meet their needs.

Clearly, if mental or cognitive processes play a part in stress, then it makes sense that there are ways to lower stress in less extreme ways than a total lifestyle change or taking medication. And, no, our emotions don't have a will of their own. They can be controlled. Self-control is listed as a fruit of the Spirit (Galatians 5:22–23). We can and must take control of our thought processes and our feelings.

FAULTY THOUGHT PATTERNS

Clearly, our mental response—our personal perception— is the crucial factor. Faulty thought patterns can intensify the effects of stress. Let's consider two specific types of faulty thought patterns: false beliefs and distorted thought processes.

False Beliefs

Christian counselor Robert McGee has identified four false beliefs that often contribute to the stresses of work and life: (1) the performance trap, (2) approval addiction, (3) the blame game, and (4) the snare of shame.[1]

Those caught in the *performance trap* believe that their success, happiness, and personal worth are wrapped up in their ability to measure up to certain standards. They feel good about themselves or about life only if they are performing at peak levels. Often we relate top performance to closing the sale, getting the raise, handling the work crisis, or securing the promotion. Yet the reality is that God made us to be human *beings,* not human *doings.* Our personal worth is not gained by being perfect or eliminating all mistakes from our lives but in rejoicing in the fact that we are imperfect, forgiven people related by faith to a perfect God. We are significant because of that relationship, not because of our performance.

In *approval addiction,* people add to their stress by seeking acceptance and approval of some other person. They must be approved by someone in order to be able to feel good about themselves. In fact, they believe that such approval is the way to their personal, lasting fulfillment and happiness. The person who falls into the performance trap becomes convinced that "I should be perfect," whereas approval addiction leads to the thought that "I must please others." The performance trap is often motivated by the fear of failure, whereas approval addiction flows naturally from the fear of rejection. Again, it is important to recognize that, if we are accepted by God and reconciled to Him, our personal worth doesn't stand or fall on the basis of whether or not we are approved by other people.

The blame game and *the snare of shame* lead to two other related false beliefs. Blame is a two-edged sword that condemns anyone who fails, whether ourself or someone else. The snare of shame causes the individual to conclude that life is hopeless because of some failure or blot on his life or record. *I will never be worth anything,* she tells herself.

These core beliefs, faulty though they are, affect many of us and strongly compound our stresses because they guide our responses to the adversities of life.

Distorted Thought Processes

These can be further complicated by distorted thought processes. You may be wondering how a thought process can produce stress. It probably happens the same way distorted glasses produce a headache. Some time ago I began realizing that I was experiencing more headaches than usual. My physician suggested it might be time to have my glasses checked. It had been almost three years since my glasses had been changed, and my vision had changed significantly. Because I was straining to see things through the distortion caused by incorrect prescription lenses, I had begun having headaches. In the same way, when we try to see the world through distorted thought processes, we compound the stress we experience.

Chris Thurman described four of these distorted thinking patterns. One of the most common is what we might call *magnification*, or making a mountain out of a molehill. As Chris and I talked about magnification and increased stress, we realized that it affected us in different but similar ways.

Chris is a skilled tennis player. For him to miss an easy shot is enough to, as he put it, "yank my chain and cause me to see red. I make a fifty-dollar event out of a fifty-cent miss." For myself, I tend to magnify missed, self-imposed deadlines. Frequently I set a goal to finish a certain project by a certain time, often far earlier than when the project actually has to be completed. No one else might even be aware of the deadline. But for me, missing that deadline seems like a disaster.

What hill do you find yourself frequently making a mountain out of? Could it be getting to the copier just after one of the secretaries has started running off a fifty-page project? Or is it being asked to cut five minutes off your break to attend a work-safety meeting? It's important that we recognize when we are indeed making a mountain out of a molehill and cut the problem down to size.

Polarization is a second major distorted thought process. Sometimes known as black-and-white thinking, it's a way of slicing reality into all-or-nothing extremes. When we polarize, either the event was absolutely great, or it was terrible, awful, and catastrophic. We see some individuals as total good guys and others as absolute bad guys.

Unfortunately, people tend to allow black-and-white thinking to go to one of two extremes. Sometimes they have trouble seeing issues as black-and-white that the Bible labels as such. On the other hand, they may try to turn everything into a black-and-white issue and wind up adopting a legalistic approach to life. This kind of thinking is what leads people to the conclusion that "I failed, therefore I must be a failure. I didn't get the project done on time. I didn't bring my department in under budget. I didn't meet my quota of widgets on the production line today, so I'm a terrible, no-good person." One of the most important insights we can gain in life is an understanding of which issues the Bible labels as black-and-white and which ones it doesn't.

Selective abstraction is another stress-producing way of distorted thinking. This involves focusing on one small factor or incident to the exclusion of everything else. Sometimes we call it "missing the forest for the trees." Some time ago my friend John, who had just secured a new job with an up-and-coming company, met me for coffee. He was so low he was reaching up to touch bottom.

"What happened?" I asked.

"I just totally blew it, Don. I love this job, but now I may get fired."

"What happened?" I asked again.

"Well, I was at this meeting in the conference room with my boss and our biggest client. I reached over to pick up a pen and knocked over my coffee cup. Spilt coffee on the client —even got some on my boss. He's a perfectionist, and I know he can't stand people who do stupid things like that. He's probably thinking of firing me."

It is crucial for us to learn to keep our eyes on the big picture and not get lost in the details. Beware the danger of focusing on one small negative that really doesn't matter when weighed against the overall positive picture.

Overgeneralization is a fourth distortion in our thought processes that may intensify stress in our work life. This thought distortion often involves the words *always* or *never.* Thurman labels it the "history always repeats itself" distortion. It is a common one in marriage relationships and at the workplace as well.

Often we overgeneralize about relationships at work, getting along with the boss, or even new technology. "This new computer system is just a total impossibility," Betty insisted. "I'll never get the hang of using it. Why did they invent these things anyway? Just to make it difficult for us?"

Six months later I stopped by the office where Betty works. "So, you're still here," I pointed out, smiling. "Does that mean the computer is gone?"

"No," she said. "I have actually learned to coexist with it. It is not what I would call a peaceful coexistence, but I have survived. I didn't think I would ever learn to use this system. Typing was one thing, but getting a handle on using a word processor was something else. Now I can deal with it."

What are some of the areas you have found yourself overgeneralizing? Did you let a couple of incidents convince you that a certain fellow worker is impossible to get along with? Have the new policies and procedures left you feeling that you have no future with the company? Remember, things may not be working out very well for you right now, but there is always tomorrow—or even the next day.

CHOOSING A DIFFERENT RESPONSE

So how can I change my way of responding to stressful circumstances? Perhaps the first thing to do is look at my pattern of thinking in a given situation and compare it with these false beliefs and distorted thought processes. I need to ask myself, *Have I fallen into one of the false beliefs? Am I basing my worth on performance or approval? Or am I overgeneralizing or making a mountain out of a molehill? Have I been guilty of black-and-white thinking in a "shades of gray" situation?*

Once I've evaluated my thought processes in this way, I can adjust to a more healthy pattern of thought. I look at the situation and what I am thinking about and honestly ask myself, *What am I telling myself about this situation? How do I feel about it, and how am I responding?* Then I look beyond my immediate feelings and thoughts to ask, *What are the basic beliefs on which my response to this situation is based? Are they false beliefs, or are they valid? What about my thought processes? Are they faulty in some way?*

Next I look for ways to replace faulty thought processes or false beliefs with the truth. After all, as Jesus pointed out in His ministry, knowing the truth sets us free (John 8:32).

When it comes to the pressures of life, we not only can reject false beliefs and faulty thought processes, we also can control certain circumstances by tactfully saying no. Sometimes it seems as though some of us have been born with a genetic deficiency that makes it impossible for our lips to frame the simple word *no.*

Suppose your boss has asked you to do three things, any one of which is enough to max you out. You might respond by asking, "Which two of these would you like me to do? Which is most important?" or, "I'd really like to take on these new projects, but I can't without cutting back somewhere else." If you find it hard to say no, ask yourself why. Maybe you feel guilty. Or you may be afraid of conflict.

We also need to utilize such basic stress helps as exercise, rest, and proper diet and nutrients. Maybe, instead of eating coffee and donuts at break time, you need to start taking ten-minute walks. Use the stairs instead of the elevator. Or maybe you need to get into a full-blown physical-fitness improvement program. Exercise or even a brisk walk can boost energy, relieve feelings of tension, and improve blood circulation. Even moving your arms and shoulders while you're sitting at your desk can help.

Dr. Timothy Oroehrs of the Henry Ford Hospital Sleep Disorders Research Center in Detroit suggests that the average person gets from one to one and one-half hours too little sleep at night.[2] He suggests that most people need nine hours of sleep a night, and the average person's alertness is boosted by one-third by getting that extra sleep.

Eating proper foods can also help alleviate the pressures of life by producing the chemicals in the brain that increase alertness. A study of students at the Massachusetts Institute of Technology showed that proteins significantly improved their ability to do mental tasks, while carbohydrates limited students' mental abilities by making them feel more relaxed.[3]

When it comes to diet, we need to be careful about using food to medicate pain or alleviate stress. Numerous studies have suggested that many people eat more in response to stress. Often we use food to improve our mood. When you feel the urge to eat, ask yourself, *Am I really hungry? Do I need to eat right now? Am I about to eat something that isn't really good for me?* Perhaps the alternative would be a brisk walk or listening to music. One woman in a weight-and-stress reduction program resisted the temptation to snack by walking to a nearby shop during her break and buying herself a single red rose.[4]

Another important way to deal with stress is by taking regular breaks. I have found it helpful in my personal battle with stress to occasionally take five- to ten-minute naps. I have been amazed at the amount of energy this has given me. For years we have heard how important it is to take regular breaks when driving on a long-distance trip. It seems logical to assume that the same thing would be true of our work.

A PRAYER OF SERENITY

Finally, recognize that there are certain circumstances we can change and some we can't. I found the tried and true "Serenity Prayer" to be incredibly helpful. It goes like this: *"God, grant me the serenity to accept the things I cannot change, the courage to change the things I can and the wisdom to know the difference."* Many situations seem hopeless, so we may find it helpful to work on changing our outlook or perception since we can't change the situation itself.

Consider the difference between Moses' and the Israelites' perception of their situation at the edge of the Red Sea.

The Egyptian army was in hot pursuit. Most of the Israelites considered their plight to be totally hopeless. There was no way they could conceivably escape from the mightiest military force on earth. They were convinced that Moses had led them out of Egypt only to die in this barren setting.

On the other hand, Moses was convinced that God wouldn't let them down. He didn't understand how God would deliver them, but he knew what he could do and what he would have to leave up to God. We know the result of Moses' attitude of faith: the incredible preservation of the Israelites through the Red Sea on dry ground!

We can learn a lot about the relationship between stress and control issues from the life of Moses. We must take control of what we can control, relinquish control of other things to God, and understand the difference between actual pressures and perceptions that contribute to our pressures.

If you feel stressed in your work, many of the pressures you feel are real. It is also likely that your perceptions of circumstances may be intensifying those pressures. Learn to minimize those pressures you can, change your perception where appropriate, take control of what you can, and surrender to God what you can't control.

CHAPTER SEVEN

------------------| |------------------

PRIORITIES
AND URGENCIES

I have fifteen things to do today, and they all need to get done right now. I just don't think I can take any more."

I was in the process of sweetening my coffee when I heard Cynthia's familiar voice, laced with more than a little stress. She had just come from a meeting with her boss—the executive vice president of our division. I wasn't surprised at her response. In an earlier meeting, the boss and I had talked about the fact that we had thirty-one projects, all of which corporate wanted "done right now, and done right."

Further complicating things was the failure of our courier company to deliver one of those "rush—extremely urgent" projects and a mix-up by our printer on one of the most important brochures. Plus, as I scanned my daytime planner, I realized we had several things to do to prepare for a video shoot with Tom Landry the next morning. In the meantime, I had to record an interview with world-class sprinter Carl Lewis at 3:00 that afternoon and then rush across town to host a live radio program in the studios of the USA Radio Network. What I didn't know at the time was that I would get stuck in a major traffic tie-up on LBJ Expressway and wind up slipping into my studio seat literally as the opening theme music was rolling. But such is the urgency of life today.

Our society seems to thrive on crises. Many of us find our lives ruled by the tyranny of the urgent. We need it done right now, we tell ourselves. More is faster. Faster is better.

One of our biggest obstacles seems to be interruptions— and often not things that are critical to our success. They intrude on those things that are really important, and usually make it hard for us to focus on the things that can make the most difference."

Whatever your job or responsibilities, chances are that far too many tasks—even too many people—compete for your attention. Distractions, interruptions, pressures, deadlines— everything—is urgent. I'll never forget the time, many years ago, when I was working with a team on an important radio production project. We paused midway through the afternoon to have a quick bite of lunch. I asked our executive secretary to thank the Lord for the food. When she bowed her head, she prayed the ultimate prayer of the urgent: "Lord, help us get everything done now, please, and in order. Amen." Nothing about the food or the people. The focus of the prayer, indeed the focus of all of us who were involved in the project, was "Let's get it done."

COMPLICATING FACTORS

Two factors come to mind that further complicate the intense stress produced by the tyranny of the urgent. One is what I refer to as the Rescue 911 mentality; the other is the expectations of others. The first is a more internally motivated factor; the second is externally focused.

The television series "Rescue 911," hosted by Star Trek star William Shatner, presents a series of events in which someone is injured, trapped, stranded, or otherwise caught in a desperate situation. Someone nearby dials 911, and police, fire, ambulance, or other appropriate personnel come rushing to the rescue, lights flashing and sirens blaring.

When someone has suffered a heart attack, become trapped in a burning building, or been seriously hurt in an automobile crash, a Rescue 911 mentality is totally appropriate. The problem comes when we start to live our lives from crisis to crisis. Perhaps, as Archibald Hart suggested in his book *Adrenaline and Stress*, we've become addicted to the adrenaline of the crisis. Or it may be that we have simply developed a crisis-coping approach to managing our lives and our responsibilities. We may have even reached the point of manufacturing crises when none are apparent.

Some time ago I was talking with a colleague about a mutual friend who has been quite successful as a manager. "Sam has really been feeling the effects of stress," my friend told me. "He has been to the doctor with digestive problems and even had some chest pains. Well, I'm not surprised. He treats everything as though it was super urgent. In fact, when he and I served on a committee together, it seemed like every letter or memo I received from him was urgent. Every phone message contained the same thing. Not only that, he's the kind of person who wants to try to bail everybody else out, solve their problems, pull all the loose ends together."

I suggested that it sounded like our friend's life resembled a series of episodes from "Rescue 911." He nodded agreement. "It certainly seems to be his most common approach to his work, at least from my perspective."

The other complicating factor—the expectations of other people—affects some occupations more than others. Most all of us have someone (either a boss if you are an employee, or your customers and clients if you are the boss) who expects us to do our job and do it well. But for some highly visible individuals, measurable statistics and success add incredible pressures that compound the tyranny of the urgent.

My wife and I reside in Lincoln, Nebraska. Every morning on my way to work at Back to the Bible I drive past Memorial Stadium, home of the 1994 National Champion Nebraska Cornhuskers football team. Coincidentally, I grew up, and my parents still live, just a few miles from Legion Field, the site of many home football games of the 1993 National Champions, the Alabama Crimson Tide. For a number of years I lived in Dallas, home of the 1993 and 1994 Super Bowl Champion Dallas Cowboys.

Recently I toured the athletic facilities at the University of Nebraska. Symbols of success were everywhere—the 1994 National Championship trophy, prominently displayed outside Coach Tom Osborne's office, plus numerous other trophies from previous national championships, a couple of Heismann trophies, and a plethora of Big Eight championship trophies. However, a telling question from one of our group demonstrated the incredible pressure to get to the top and to stay there: "It's a beautiful trophy, and you've displayed it well. But where will you put next year's trophy?" That's the kind of pressure that head coaches can relate to firsthand. Not only are you supposed to do a good job and play by the rules, but you need to win—win early and often, win right away, and win it all. As NBA superstar Michael Jordan told one sportswriter, "Winning it all is what counts."

Public servants face the same kind of pressure. At the recent dedication of the new international headquarters of Back to the Bible, I had the opportunity to talk with Lincoln mayor Mike Johanns, who has received bipartisan acknowledgment for doing a good job. He commented, however, that "people certainly notice when crime statistics are up or we don't land a major new industry." The mayor and I had been discussing the fact that the murder rate for Lincoln had climbed 30 percent from the past year—four murders recorded instead of three. He laughed when I told him that a relatively crime-free weekend in our former city of residence, Dallas, was when only three or four murders took place.

Just a few months before, my wife and I were talking with Houston Police Chief Sam Nuchia and his wife, Liz, at a marriage-enrichment seminar we conducted for members of the Houston Police Department. Liz Nuchia's voice took on a

STRESS TEST

Doing It Now

To what extent do you feel you "need it done right now," that "More is faster" and "Faster is better"? Take the following stress test to see whether the urgent overrules the significant in your life, adding to stress. Choose a number from 1 to 5 and put it in the blank in front of each statement, using this scale: 1 = not at all; 2 = rarely; 3 = sometimes; 4 = often; 5 = most of the time.

_____ 1. *I live my days from crisis to crisis.*

_____ 2. *I try to please people in my work, even if it means extra projects or long hours.*

_____ 3. *At home, I do lots of little urgent things rather than focus on a couple of major projects that are significant (the "big stones").*

_____ 4. *I do not evaluate my goals in terms of how they will relate to loving God wholeheartedly and loving people unconditionally.*

_____ 5. *I measure my success by what people say about my job performance.*

SCORING:
     1–11 Your priorities are largely right.
     12–15 The urgent is wooing you.
     16–20 The urgent is winning against the important.
     21–25 The urgent is your tyrant!

....

passionate tone as she talked about the pressures on her husband. "The crime rate increases or some incident happens with one of the officers, and they blame it all on Sam. They don't give him credit for the good things he does, the hard work he puts in, or all the pressures he faces. If the crime rate is up, if more murders are committed, it's all his fault."

In the ministry, similar pressures can compound the stresses of pastors and pastors' wives. Kathy and I spent nineteen years in pastoral ministry. We have seen firsthand the urgency of that phone call to visit someone in the hospital or to talk with a parishioner's dying relative. My wife recently reminded me of the time I received a phone call at 1:00 A.M. from someone who felt that it was important for me to come to the hospital to be with him while his wife delivered their baby. Ironically, this couple had left our church several months before in a huff because the church wasn't living up to their expectations. I was reminded of two pastor friends who, laboring under difficult circumstances and shrinking congregations, were asked to leave because "the work just wasn't growing under their ministry."

PRIORITY PRINCIPLE

So how do we counter the tyranny of the urgent—the Rescue 911 mentality and the expectations of others? One of the keys—and a major way to address stress in the workplace and in life—is found in the title and a section title of a book coauthored by management expert Stephen Covey: *First Things First*. The title of Section Two reads:

THE MAIN THING IS TO KEEP THE MAIN THING THE MAIN THING

In other words, living by priorities is the antidote to the stress generated by the tyranny of urgencies.

I suspect at this point that some of you are skeptical: "Sure, Don, you're right. Just put first things first, everything will work out." I'm not surprised at your response, but stay with me. I think you'll see the benefits.

Listen to a story I heard Stephen Covey tell at a seminar several months ago. One of Covey's associates had heard it at a seminar he attended. I found it to have an incredible impact on the way I dealt with the stresses and decisions I face.

At the seminar in question, the instructor said, "It's time for a quiz."[1] He reached under the table and pulled out a wide-mouthed gallon jar, setting it on the table next to a platter with a number of fist-sized rocks on it. "How many of these rocks do you think we can get into the jar?"

The seminar attendees made their guesses. "Let's find out." He put one rock in the jar, then another and another. Finally the pile of rocks inside the jar was level with the top.

"Is the jar full?" Everyone looked at the rocks and agreed that it was.

Then the instructor pulled out a bucket of gravel. He dumped the gravel into the jar, shook it, and the gravel went into the little spaces left around the big rocks. The instructor grinned and asked, "Is the jar full yet?"

By this time the seminar attendees were on to the professor. "Probably not," they replied.

"Good." he nodded. Reaching under the table he brought out a bucket of sand and started dumping it in. The sand filled in the tiny spaces left by the rocks and the gravel. Once again, he asked, "Is the jar full?"

"No," the attendees roared.

"Good," the instructor responded. Grabbing a pitcher of water, he began to pour it in. When he had poured almost a quart of water into the jar, he asked, "What's the point?"

Someone replied, "Well, there are gaps, and, if you really work at it, you can always fit more into your life."

"No," the instructor said. "That's not the point. The point is this: If you hadn't put those big rocks in first, would you ever have gotten any of them in?"

When I first read *First Things First*, I was intrigued by the story, but my first impression was exactly like that of the attendee. In fact, to a large degree, that was the premise on which I had operated. There are always little time gaps, and if you work hard, work efficiently, plan your work, and work your plan, you can always cram more into your life. I had worked at shuffling my schedule, managing my time, delegating things to others, canceling or postponing certain activities, always working toward the goal of finding time to do those things that are really important. But I've never been able to escape the tyranny of the urgent.

To be candid, I still struggle with this issue. But I have finally come to realize the importance of putting the big rocks in first. I'm convinced that the two "big rocks" in the Bible, the ultimate priorities God has given us, are loving God with all our heart and loving our neighbor as ourself. I like to phrase them as wholehearted love for God and unconditional love for people.

Jesus gave this two-fold mandate during His final week, and it came on the heels of intense questioning and confrontations between the Master and the religious authorities of His day. One of the scribes, having listened to the dialogue and realizing that Jesus did have the answers, asked, "Which is the first commandment of all?" (Mark 12:28). In other words, what is the ultimate priority? For Jewish people in first-century Palestine, the commandments were the ultimate governing force in life. So Jesus' response didn't surprise anybody; it simply underscored what they had heard Him say before.

From Jesus' perspective, the first of the commandments was the familiar *Shema* (see Deuteronomy 6:4–5): "Hear, O Israel, the Lord our God, the Lord is one. And you shall love the Lord your God with all your heart, with all your soul, with all your mind, and with all your strength" (Mark 12:29–30). The second commandment, following close and like the first, is "You shall love your neighbor as yourself" (v. 31). This command is from Leviticus 19:18. There is no other commandment greater than these.

Some years ago I spent about a week of vacation time searching through the Old and New Testaments to confirm my suspicion that every biblical mandate relates to these in some fashion or another. I became convinced that these priorities represent the lowest common denominators for living the way God intended. All the other rocks, the sand, and the gravel we put into the jar of our life must be related to them.

In essence, everything I do in life, every relationship I have, every objective I set, everything I devote my attention to should be evaluated in terms of how it will relate to my loving God wholeheartedly and loving people unconditionally. That brings me to the subject of the urgent versus the important.

As I read Stephen Covey's *First Things First*, then attended his seminar, I began to realize just how powerfully we are all affected by urgencies, whether it's the sound of a beeper or portable telephone, the knock at the door interrupting a quiet evening, the pressing deadline of income taxes, or a friend who says, "I really need your help." All these things are urgent. The question is, Are they also important?

According to Stephen Covey, the two primary factors that drive our choices about how we use our time are urgency and importance.[2] Many things, such as picking up a visiting executive from a hotel for our boss or filling that extra set of orders that came in past the deadline at the end of the day fit the urgent category. Others, such as physical exercise, personal devotions, or time with individual children, fit into the important. We know we need to do them, but in the press of the urgent we let them go.

Sitting in a basket on my desk right now are two projects. One is an article I hope to write, the other a proposal that could remove some financial pressure from my radio ministry by adding an underwriter. I consider both these things important. So far, I've allowed the pressure of the urgent to keep me from doing them. I say "I've allowed" because it isn't merely the pressures that have kept me from doing them, it's the choices I've made.

My friend Zig Ziglar, who enjoys eating in cafeterias, draws an accurate parallel between the wide variety of choices in the food line of a cafeteria and the choices we make in life. "We need to choose," he says, "and the choices we make will ultimately determine how successful we are."[3]

Some time ago at the beginning of a new year, Zig Ziglar sat down and made a list of a variety of things he wanted to do, including conducting family seminars, recording a short daily radio program, playing golf regularly, writing, exercising, and traveling. His conclusion was that, if he took the time to do everything he wanted to do, even if there were no interruptions, and he still slept at least seven hours a night, it would take more than three hundred hours a week—far more than the one hundred sixty-eight hours available—to fulfill just those goals. "I had to eliminate much of the good so I could choose the best, just as I do in the cafeteria line."[4]

To return to Covey's analogy, everything in life is either urgent or not urgent, important or unimportant. Thus, he divides all the decisions we make into four categories or "quadrants."[5] Some he labels as both urgent and important, like pressing problems, deadline-driven projects, or crises (Quadrant 1). Others are important, but not urgent (Quadrant 2). They include planning, relationship building, preparation, clarifying our values, and empowering others. The third category—urgent but not important—includes interruptions, some phone calls, mail, reports of meetings, and popular activities. Into the fourth category—neither urgent nor important—he places trivia, busy work, junk mail, and time wasters.

One of the most valuable contributions of Stephen Covey and the big rocks story is to urge us to move from the pressures, deadlines, irate clients, and broken equipment of Quadrant 1 to the long-range planning, interactive empowering, and skill enhancement of Quadrant 2.

When you examine the public career of Jesus, it is clear that His life provides the perfect balance between dealing with the urgent and maintaining the priority of the important. After what most Bible scholars have labeled "the single busiest day of His entire ministry" (Mark 1:16–34)—a day in which He called disciples, taught in the synagogue, cast out a demon, healed a seriously ill woman, and ministered to an entire city—Jesus awakened well before daylight the next morning, went out to a solitary place, and prayed (v. 35).

Later, Peter and the other disciples tracked Him down and said, "Everyone is looking for you." Jesus didn't say, "I don't have time for them." But He did make sure He had time for that most important activity of prayer and fellowship with His Father. Having done so, He told Simon and the others, "Let us go into the next towns, that I may preach there also, because for this purpose I have come forth" (v. 38).

Throughout His life, Jesus maintained that critical balance between the urgent and the important. He never carried a pager, wore a watch, or stayed in contact through modern technologies, yet He was always on time and always found the time to do what mattered. And those things that He focused on always seemed to reflect the value of loving His Father and loving people. Two incidents illustrate this well.

In the first, Jesus' friend Lazarus became extremely ill, and Mary and Martha sent word to the Lord to come at once, because they were convinced that He could heal Lazarus (John 11:1–4). John is careful to note that "Jesus loved Martha and her sister and Lazarus," but He stayed two more days where He was after hearing of Lazarus's illness (vv. 5–6).

When Jesus finally arrived in Bethany, Martha's comment, "Lord, if you had been here, my brother would not have died" (v. 21), contained an implicit rebuke. But Jesus had already told His disciples that "Lazarus is dead. And I am glad for your sakes that I was not there, that you may believe" (vv. 14–15). Even though neither the sisters nor the disciples understood fully what was happening, Jesus governed His choices and His timing by an ultimate overriding purpose to motivate the people He loved to lovingly trust the Father He loved—and to raise His friend Lazarus from the dead.

Later in His ministry, en route to Jerusalem from Jericho, the most important mission ever undertaken in the history of the human race—His death on the cross—was interrupted by two blind beggars sitting beside the road who cried out, "Have mercy on us, O Lord, Son of David!" (Matthew 20:30). As their cries persisted, Jesus paused and asked, "What do you want Me to do for you?" Compassionately He met their request to have their sight restored, then immediately resumed His trip to Jerusalem—and they followed Him. Again we observe the perfect balance between fulfilling the ultimate priority and being available to meet an urgent need, not allowing that need to hinder the more important purpose.

From the perspective of Stephen Covey and others, establishing priorities is closely connected to values and principles. Covey uses the analogy of the compass to point us to the importance of establishing what he calls "true north principles." From Covey's perspective, these principles go beyond values, even beyond practices and religion.[6] They boil down to what he refers to as the Law of the Farm—a law he suggests governs every arena of life. It is the law of sowing and reaping, of character and integrity, the same principle Paul pointed to in Galatians 6:7–9. "Do not be deceived. God is not mocked; for whatever a man sows, that will he also reap. . . . Let us not grow weary while doing good, for in due season we shall reap if we do not lose heart."

The good and valid aspect of what Covey says is that the Law of the Farm—the law of sowing and reaping, the law of long-term values rather than quick-fix solutions, cramming-more-into-less strategies—is what really works. The weakness, as I perceive it, of Covey's perspective is that he and others fall into the trap of ignoring what is ultimately "true north"—biblical absolutes. Covey doesn't point to Christ or the Bible but to what he labels true-north principles based on his view of human conscience. Almost anyone who has studied human nature will concede that there are times when conscience will steer us in the wrong direction. Covey's thesis is that conscience is "the factor that will always point to true north."[7] The flaw of this thesis can be seen in the fact that even the gadget we label the compass, which generally points in a northerly direction, can be drawn to point in other directions by magnetic influences. Furthermore, magnetic north is not the same as "true north."

Covey's work reminded me of Carl Menniger's excellent book *Whatever Became of Sin?* It accurately identified the foundational human problem yet failed to point to the ultimate biblical solution found in Jesus Christ.

URGENT OR IMPORTANT?

Throughout life—in big decisions and small—we make choices based on what we value most. For some of us, it's the urgency of the moment that overrides other factors. At other times, it may be the social expectations of others, the influence of our past, the desire to fulfill our personal agenda, or a compulsion to avoid physical or emotional pain. My goal is to move us from making decisions based on the urgent to increasingly making those choices based on important biblically based values, firmly rooted in those two ultimate priorities of loving God wholeheartedly and loving people unconditionally. Since my assumption is that Scripture speaks to the issue of principle-based or priority-based living, it will be helpful to examine what Scripture says about priorities.

Early in His ministry, in the Sermon on the Mount, Jesus spoke to the issue of distractions and interruptions. He had already addressed the issue of what God expected when He pointed out that "unless your righteousness exceeds the righteousness of the scribes and Pharisees, you will by no means enter the kingdom of Heaven" (Matthew 5:20). He established the importance of laying up treasures in heaven—in other words, investing in that which is of lasting or eternal consequence—rather than simply accumulating treasures on earth, where theft and corruption put material possessions at risk (6:19–20). And He had established the premise that no one can fully serve two masters, particularly not God and material wealth (v. 24). Then, He had addressed the issue of distracting anxieties (the very term translated "anxiety" means a distraction or division of the mind), explaining the principle that allows anyone to make effective priority choices. "But seek first the kingdom of God and His righteousness, and all these things shall be added to you" (v. 33).

The religious leaders of Jesus' day had devised a carefully crafted system for making the choices necessary to govern their lives. However, as the Lord pointed out throughout His Sermon on the Mount, their approach was to make decisions based on external perception and appearance. In their system murder and adultery were wrong, but internal lust and hatred were acceptable. Loving your neighbor was required, but it was permissible to hate your enemy. Though charitable deeds and prayer were to be put on public exhibit, they didn't have to affect the greed, materialism, and hostility on the inside.

Instead, Jesus called for His listeners to make God's kingdom and righteousness a priority. His kingdom involved His authority expressed in every facet of life, while His righteousness involved a standard that went far beyond external human laws to the integrity and character that needed to be at the core of the human soul.

The key to understanding what Jesus meant by the words *seek first* can be seen in how the word *seek* was used by Mary and Joseph when their twelve-year-old son turned up missing following a trip to Jerusalem. Their approach was not at all casual. It involved an intense effort, setting aside other interests or concerns, including Joseph's work and Mary's schedule. They used all the abilities, mental and physical, that God had given them. And ultimately they succeeded in finding Him.

The practical application for us is to make living by the principles God's Word has laid down the focus in our lives. Jesus' priority mandate can keep us from worrying about personal possessions, pursuing the appearances and values of others around us, or even becoming anxious about tomorrow. Instead, as we become more goals-driven and as our goals and values correspond to what is biblical, we find ourselves less frequently distracted.

The principle here is that of streamlining, which is used with aircraft, bullet trains, and other vehicles of modern travel. Even the large eighteen-wheel trucks that roar across our interstate highway system include carefully designed baffling to cut down on wind resistance. The principle is simple: the less the resistance, the more effectively and efficiently the ultimate goal of the train, plane, or truck can be fulfilled.

According to the authors of *In Search of Excellence,* America's best-run companies have learned this kind of streamlined, values-driven priority focus. They have identified key principles, which will make their corporations distinctively successful. Companies should operate on a few "core values they hold dear," avoid getting caught up in messy bureaucracy, passionately hold to their core beliefs, and "stick to the knitting" of what they do well, with a values-driven, hands-on management approach resting on a basic philosophy.[8] The most common denominator in the values adopted by these successful companies is a focus on people—both customers and those involved in the company itself.

The lessons for our personal lives are consistent with the biblical mandate to make our relationships with God and people our priority. The more we focus on what is truly important, the less we will be distracted by those things that tug, distract, and pull at us.

Professor D. Eugene Griessman of Georgia Tech, a time management expert and author of the book *Time Tactics of Very Successful People,* interviewed hundreds of high achievers, including Bernie Marcus, the chairman of Home Depot, communications magnate Ted Turner, and Helen Gurley Brown. He emphasized that the number-one way all the "high achievers" dealt with workplace stress was by establishing priorities and sticking with them.[9] According to Griessman, Brown, the editor of *Cosmopolitan* magazine, keeps a copy of the magazine on her desk. When she is tempted to fritter away time on an activity that doesn't contribute directly to the magazine, a glance at the copy on her desk helps her get back on track.

Griessman also points to the importance of decisiveness as a tool to cut down on stress. The decision-making process can be boiled down to three steps: understand the objective, look at alternatives, and consider the risks.

David was a man who went from success in shepherding to success as a king. Despite his failures, he was recognized as a man after God's own heart. David expressed his philosophy and priorities in the statement, "One thing I have desired of the Lord, that will I seek: That I may dwell in the house of the Lord all the days of my life, to behold the beauty of the Lord, and to inquire in His temple" (Psalm 27:4).

From David's perspective, loving God wholeheartedly was the most important aspect of his life. Though as shepherd, warrior, and king he found himself pressed in life by many things, and though at times he suffered spiritual lapses, his life-long priority was to maintain fellowship with God, to see God's beauty, and to continue learning and growing.

In the New Testament the apostle Paul modeled the priorities he adopted when he abandoned Pharisaism to follow Christ. In drawing a sharp contrast between his Pharisaic pedigree and his shift in priorities when he came to faith, he points out, "I do not count myself to have apprehended; but one thing I do, forgetting those things which are behind and reaching forward to those things which are ahead, I press toward the goal for the prize of the upward call of God in Christ Jesus" (Philippians 3:13–14). The essence of what Paul is saying is that none of us has arrived. Every one of us needs to have focus, and the ultimate goal toward which we are to be focused is our relationship with Jesus Christ. This, Paul points out, is the attitude of maturity in the faith (v. 15).

Interestingly, the word *goal* in Philippians 3:14 is from the Greek word *skopos*, which comes from an unusual verb meaning to watch out for or to pay attention to. The noun speaks of a mark on which to focus the eye. Our English word "scope" comes from *skopos*. Whether a telescope used by an astronomer to view the rings of Saturn, a microscope used by a biologist to learn the specific bacteria causing a certain disease, or even a scope mounted on the rifle of the hunter in search of deer or elk, the concept is the same. The scope enables us to focus beyond the distractions and clutter of the urgent on that which we value or consider important.

ADVICE FOR MARTHA

Perhaps no person in Scripture provides as practical an illustration of how establishing the right priorities can help us deal with the stress of urgencies as does Martha, the sister of Lazarus. Early in Jesus' career, Martha had welcomed Jesus to her house (Luke 10:38–42). During this visit Martha's sister Mary sat at Jesus' feet and listened to His word, but Martha was distracted—drawn around or tied up in knots—with much serving, focused on the stress of her workplace (her home). Martha must have felt the press of having to feed at least sixteen, one of whom was a perfect person. Think about Martha's personality. I've observed seven aspects of Martha's problem.

First, she wanted to be in control. It was her house, or at least that's how Luke identified it, and she was the one who wanted this meal to turn out just right.

In addition to her control issues, she was a task-oriented person. Perhaps Martha would have considered it a waste of time to sit at Jesus' feet and listen. After all, if you don't get things done, where is your value?

Furthermore, Martha was probably more than a little competitive. After all, this was her sister sitting at Jesus' feet. If she couldn't sit and listen—and she certainly didn't have the time—she sure wasn't going to let her sister.

Fourth, Martha loved to give advice. You don't find her asking questions of Jesus, listening to Him, or even learning from others. Martha's approach was to give advice. Picture the scene later before Lazarus's tomb. Jesus tells the men nearby to roll away the stone. Martha hastily interrupts, "Lord, don't you understand? There's a terrible stink. He's been dead four days" (see John 11:39). Jesus was only the

Creator of the Universe. How incongruous for one who knew so little as Martha to advise Him!

Fifth, Martha struggled with anger, like a pot simmering. She was about to boil over. You can almost cut the anger in her words: "Lord, do You not care that my sister has left me to serve alone? Therefore tell her to help me" (Luke 10:40). Frequently our stresses lead to anger.

Sixth, Martha was plagued by anxiety and inner turmoil. Jesus pointed out to her how worried she was, troubled about many things (see Luke 11:41–42). Many times I've observed Marthas of both sexes in the modern workplace, distracted by first one thing and then another, physically and emotionally drained by the stresses, struggling with anger over the inability to handle what they perceive to be an overwhelming demand.

This leads to the last of Martha's problems—her priorities were out of focus. We know that because of the perspective Jesus shared with her. Notice the three things He pointed out to her and their applications for us today.

First, Jesus might have said, "Martha, you're not paying attention to me." This is implied in the fact that He called her name twice: "Martha, Martha." Many times when we fail to establish and live by priorities, we are so torn by the tyranny of the urgent that we can't even hear or see the importance of refocusing and reprioritizing. It may take a whole lot to get our attention. I remember hearing the story of a man who set out with the goal of making a million dollars. He poured literally everything he had into that goal. Finally, when he had achieved it, he was able to enjoy it only for a short time, because his wife left him, took their two young children, and filed for divorce. Sometimes we are just not paying attention.

Another thing Jesus might have told Martha was, "Martha, you have too many irons in the fire. You're worried and troubled about many things. Your mind is divided, your thoughts stirred up and agitated." The words Jesus used in Luke 10:41 draw a vivid picture of someone who cannot concentrate, who feels the physical and mental agitation of stress. That's where Martha was—and where many of us are. Jesus pointed out the reason: "Martha, you've neglected what matters most and is best. One thing is needed" (see v. 42). He told her three things about this priority: it was needed, it was good, and it was of lasting value—it would not be taken away.

In the final anaysis, it came down to a choice. Mary opted for what mattered, and her choice to sit at Jesus' feet and listen to Him certainly fit the ultimate priority of loving God wholeheartedly and loving people unconditionally.

The question is, "Have you learned to operate by putting the big rocks in your jar first, or do you still find it easy to get distracted by the tyranny of the urgent, the mentality of 'Rescue 911,' or the need to win the approval of others?" Let's learn a lesson from Martha and Paul and David, a lesson repeated by motivational experts such as Stephen Covey, Zig Ziglar, Thomas Peters, and Robert Waterman. Let's learn to put first things first—to make the main thing the main thing.

CHAPTER EIGHT

PERSONALITIES (YOURS AND OTHERS)

F loyd, my college roommate, used to sing at the top of his lungs, "What a wonderful world this would be, if everybody were just like me." There were only two problems when Floyd sang that song. For one thing, Floyd couldn't carry a tune in a bushel basket. The other problem was with the content of his song. I think the world would be a terribly boring place if everyone were just like Floyd—or, for that matter, just like you or me.

The fact is, God has made each of us different. Those differences are part of the value we find in God's incredibly varied universe. They can also be the source of a great deal of stress, particularly in our work.

Some time ago, when I served as the chief operating officer for a large parachurch organization, I chaired a weekly meeting of our management council. This group included a take-charge physician, an outgoing marketing individual, a "by-the-book" chief financial officer, and an "our mission is to help people" therapist, among others. Almost every meeting was guaranteed to produce what we referred to as spirited, in-depth discussions. Sometimes the sparks would fly. During one particularly heated interchange one of the members of our council threw up her hands and said, "Ours must be a dysfunctional company!"

There's not a company or a family that isn't dysfunctional to some degree. The fall of Adam ensured that. In fact, most of the stress we face in work and life comes from interacting with people, some of whom are very much like us, whereas others are as different from us as day is from night.

PERSONALITY THEORIES

Hippocrates, who lived in Greece about four centuries before Christ, has been recognized as the father of modern medicine. He began noticing how the patients he treated seemed to have different temperaments that led to different behavior patterns. Some seemed to have strong leadership traits and demonstrated a tendency to take charge; others were more fun-loving, loud, talkative, and personable; still others wanted everything organized just so and at times were moody; still others appeared to be more passive and easygoing.

As Hippocrates began studying these personalities, he came up with four labels, based on the bodily fluids he believed to be the source of these different temperaments. He called the more outgoing, high-energy, and optimistic individuals *sanguine*, which means blood. Those he called *choleric*, the word for yellow bile, struggled with anger and control issues. He felt that those who were *melancholy*—described by black bile—seemed to have greater intelligence and a tendency toward depression. His final classification, *phlegmatic*, from human phlegm, denoted those who were passive and peaceful.[1]

Although the connection with bodily fluids has long since been discarded, these basic personality patterns, although described in different ways, continue to be observed and catalogued by those who study the way human beings interact. For example, the choleric, sanguine, phlegmatic, and melancholic temperament labels are still used by Tim LaHaye,[2] Florence Littauer, and others.

Another common way of looking at personality differences, popularized by Christian psychiatrists Frank Minirth and Paul Meier, is to view different personal tendencies by using commonly accepted personality labels from psychiatry. Using this view, individuals who exhibit perfectionistic traits are seen as more obsessive-compulsive than those who are more outgoing and personable, who are called hysterical. Those with strong controlling tendencies might be considered paranoid, while those who take a casual live-and-let-live approach might be considered more passive, or even passive-aggressive.[3] Those who hold this view are careful to distinguish between personality traits or tendencies and the full-blown personality disorders.

Still another recent development in looking at personalities was put together by Katharine Briggs and her daughter, Isabel Myers, who based much of their Myers-Briggs type indicator on Carl Jung's book *Psychological Types*.[4] The Myers Briggs approach uses a series of questions to determine four basic personality types in pairs. The first pair is the familiar extrovert or introvert; the second, the sensate—who gathers data through the senses—or intuitive; the third, the thinker or the feeler; and the fourth, the judge—more structured and planned—or the perceiver. Frequently the Myers-Briggs approach classifies individuals based on sensate-intuitive or thinker-feeler categories. For example, the sensate thinker is viewed as more practical and able to handle technical tasks better, whereas the sensate feeler may be more concerned with reaching out to help others. The intuitive thinker is likely to be a more big-picture, future-oriented individual, whereas the intuitive feeler will be more idealistic.

Still another way of viewing the personalities was developed by psychologist William Marston and refined by John Geier and Dorothy Downey. Their Performax© personal profile system allows a participant to analyze personal behavior in such categories as emotional tendencies, goals, the criteria he uses in judging others, the way he influences others, his perceived value to an organization, his tendency to over-use certain traits, his typical reaction under pressure, his fears, and what he needs to do to increase his effectiveness.[5] This system identifies four general categories—dominant, in-fluential, steady, and compliant—and specifies fifteen classical patterns that generally demonstrate different combinations of two of the four main behavioral styles. The dominant, like the choleric, tends to take charge. The influencing, like the san-guine, seems more outgoing and personality-oriented. The compliant resembles the phlegmatic, more easygoing per-sonality, whereas the steady, like the melancholy, tends to prefer structure and order.

WILD KINGDOM

John Trent, a Christian psychologist who has studied some thirty different instruments used to analyze the human personality has developed unique labels for these four basic personality types. His user-friendly labels include the dominant "lion," the fun-loving "otter," the structure-loving "beaver," and the easygoing, helpful "golden retriever." From Trent's perspective, the combination of these different types tends to produce what he calls a "wild kingdom" in a home or at work.

So what does all this have to do with stress in the work-place? It's simple, really. Perhaps the greatest cause of work-place stress involves clashes between different personalities. The only exception to that rule is when people of the same personality clash.

Let's go back and visit our discussion group from chapter 4. Vern, who owns several companies, has a high percentage of what we might call "lion" traits. So does Art, who works in the business owned by his father. John Trent would probably label him a "superlion."[6] Trent would likely view both Ralph, the fun-loving carpenter, and Cindy, the personable, outgoing waitress, as otters. Lynn, who runs the business she inherited from her husband, and David, the educator, are both "by-the-book" beavers, while Deena the helpful counselor and Rich the mechanic are golden retrievers.

There is no single perfect way of categorizing humans. The Bible doesn't have a personality labeling system, although I certainly appreciate the work done by Tim LaHaye, Florence Littauer, John Trent, Ken Voges, Ron Braund, and others in using biblical characters to illustrate different personality types. For example, the apostle Paul must have been a dominant/choleric/obsessive/High-D lion. He became the leader of the Christian missionary enterprise and successfully championed the grace of God before the Jerusalem Council (Acts 15). Yet he demonstrated a characteristic critical attitude toward those who did not measure up to his personal standards of excellence when he rejected Barnabas's appeal on behalf of John Mark (vv. 37–40). Peter exhibited the sanguine/influential/otter style when he walked on water. His verbal communication skills helped spark the early church, yet he vacillated on the issue of fellowship with Gentile Christians (Galatians 2:11). Abraham—a peaceful/easygoing/golden retriever patriarch—worked to restore harmony when his herdsmen clashed with those of his nephew Lot, yet he lied about Sarai his wife to avoid personal risk (Genesis 12:11–19). Moses demonstrates the perfectionistic/melancholic/steady/beaver-type personality. He showed a perfectionistic tendency to question things and even refused for a time to fill the role God gave him as spokesman for the nation of Israel before Pharaoh (Exodus 3:11–4:17).

THE PRIORITY OF RELATIONSHIPS

From God's perspective, relationships rank at the top of the priority list. I believe that's the only possible conclusion we can draw from Jesus' statement that the most important priorities in life are to love God wholeheartedly and to love people unconditionally. The essence of relationships is love, and love is far more than an emotion; it is a choice that seeks the ultimate best for the object of love. But what about those unlovable and unlovely people who do unloving things, who get in the way of your happiness and well-being and generate incredible stress in your workplace?

For example, Ralph did well at his work, but he loved to visit with people. He found that he worked much more effectively when he was part of a two- or three-man framing team. Unfortunately, Ralph had a boss—Fred—on one of his most recent projects who despised having people talk while they worked. Fred was convinced that everyone should be like him and do their best work in silence. So he made sure that Ralph worked alone and kept him isolated from other people.

Lynn, the order-and-structure, perfectionist, beaver type, often grinds her teeth over her two best salesmen, who are so good with clients they could, as she put it, "sell multiple refrigerators to Eskimos." The problem is, they never get around to documenting their sales and never take care of the paperwork. This frequently causes delays in getting financing approved for their customers and throws Lynn's carefully kept books out of kilter.

As a golden retriever, part of what makes Rich feel good about his work as a mechanic is interacting with his customers, providing them with extra help, explaining things that could go wrong or that may be starting to cause trouble, things he might notice in the process of repairing an automobile. "Cars today are complex," he likes to say. "There's so much to go wrong. If I spend some time talking with a customer, I can help him head off problems down the road." Unfortunately, Rich's boss, a powerful lion with enough dominant traits for three normal individuals, considers it a waste of Rich's time to talk with the customers. "It's against shop regulations to fraternize with the customers," he says. "Just write up the problems on the ticket." Although Rich enjoys working on cars, he sees his primary value in providing a service to people—one he feels is severely limited by his overbearing boss.

Everyone who knows him recognizes that Art is a lion, a take-charge type. After all, he is a "chip off the old block."

His dad has run the family company with an iron fist for decades, and Art has that same desire to take charge. The trouble is, he hasn't earned the respect of the people who work for the company his father started. "The mouth that roared" and the "little general" are two of the kinder ways he is often referred to by the company employees. So Art finally gave up trying to take over his dad's business and resigned himself to going into a different field. The workers threw a going-away party to celebrate his departure—and didn't invite Art!

For David, the perfectionistic, beaver-type educator who liked to teach within a carefully crafted structure, the two most frustrating points in his career happened almost simultaneously. He was demoted to junior high school where, as he put it, "they ought to take the kids out for a year and lock them up until they learn how to behave." And he was transferred to a school where the principal was a fun-loving otter who didn't care at all about structure but wanted to please the parents who were always complaining about the way David disciplined the kids in his class.

Maybe you've encountered similar kinds of frustrating situations—a boss who stifles your creativity or who gives you work to do and never thinks to ask you about it; a colleague who has absolutely no interest in details and who consequently puts an entire project at risk. Or it may be an employee whose rigid approach to doing things by the book is actually harming relationships with your clients.

WEAKNESSES: OURS AND THEIRS

There are actually two aspects to this kind of problem: one that is easy to recognize and one we'd rather pretend doesn't exist. The first involves the personality weaknesses and differences of your fellow workers, your boss, and your customers. The other, far less pleasant to acknowledge but even more crucial, involves your own personality weaknesses.

Ironically, as Trent often points out, most of our weaknesses involve strengths taken to an extreme. Solomon, the wisest human ever, pointed out that "a wise man is strong, yes, a man of knowledge increases strength" (Proverbs 24:5). The literal Hebrew wording of this proverb indicates that a wise, knowing individual will actually work to strengthen his strengths, which can help keep them in balance rather than allowing them to become extreme. One of the keys to getting along with others and thereby minimizing personality-related stress in the workplace involves sharpening or honing our own strengths while gaining a better understanding of the strengths of others.

This means being able to observe and understand different personality types. For example, powerful or dominant individuals motivated by control issues may tend to view having to submit to someone else's authority as a loss of control. This could lead to a major confrontation or even a breakdown in communications. Furthermore, individuals of this type seldom handle boring routine well; they typically prefer well-defined goals and stretching challenges.

Whenever powerful people need to be confronted—and sometimes confrontation is necessary—the best approach is to "show them how their actions affect you" and underscore mutually beneficial goals.[7] In addition, they appreciate bottom-line communication. They are not interested in a wealth of detail; instead, they prefer to "get to the point."

On the other hand, a perfectionistic or steady person typically raises many questions and wants to know the answers to individual details. Under stress this person needs reassurance, order, and structure. Such individuals may take a pessimistic, even hopeless, view of things, and that can be extremely frustrating to the more positive, popular type and even the goal-oriented, powerful personality. The steady or perfectionistic beavers need detailed information, reassurance, and support. They often have trouble with rapid changes or surprises. Specifics are essential for them, and it is important to recognize that they are conscientious individuals who are strongly committed to high standards and who by virtue of their personality will often tend to view things in a more pessimistic way.

Bob, for example, had served Vern for many years as chief financial officer and accountant of his company. Vern also was the source of a great deal of frustration, since, as an entrepreneur, Vern was always looking to put together new business ventures. Bob constantly felt frustrated because of Vern's quick, intuitive decision-making process, in contrast to Bob's style of being careful to gather enough data to make wise business decisions. Furthermore, Bob expressed an almost constant lament over the status of Vern's finances, warning, "You'll go bankrupt this time. I know you've made out OK before, but this time things will be different."

Some years ago, when I managed a Christian radio station, that the individual to whom I answered was a by-the-book beaver type who tended to be quite cautious and concerned over finances. We began every fiscal year with three relatively lean months, followed by our major fund-raising effort, which invariably put us "over the top" for the fiscal year. Every year during those first three months he'd warn, "You're not making your budget; you'll never come out in the black." At times I was urged to cut personnel or make other major budget cuts. Each time I would request permission to postpone any drastic actions until after our major fund-raiser. I came to the conclusion that the bottom-line issue wasn't finances, it was a difference in personalities, a different way of looking at things. Nor was it simply an "I'm right and he's wrong" perspective. I needed the caution of my somewhat perfectionistic colleague, and he needed the influence of my optimism and entrepreneurial spirit. Ironically, in other areas he tended to be quite optimistic as well—and in some areas I've been known to demonstrate perfectionistic traits.

This underscores yet another complicating factor. Few of us always demonstrate one specific kind of personality trait. For the most part we are a combination, often with one trait dominant, another secondary, and the other two in lesser quantity. Generally, each of us will have some of all four of the major types. Understanding this about ourselves and those we work with can help us when we see somebody who seems to have reversed roles and is acting in a manner inconsistent with what we have perceived him to be.

Personalities that don't like change are the compliant or peaceful type. They find security in the status quo and need time to adjust to changes. They also need to identify with a group, and they prefer harmony to conflict or dissension. Whereas powerful individuals often thrive on conflict and seem to go out of their way to produce it, compliant or peaceful individuals usually avoid conflict at all costs.

Another common trait of this personality is a strong tendency to show loyalty and support for those they respect. Unlike the more popular otter personality, the golden retriever will have fewer friends, but those friends are usually of the closer, more intimate variety.

Dana arrived at work one day to discover that the small counseling organization she worked for had been merged into a larger system. Before long a new administrator was in place, one who made numerous changes—none of which Dana viewed as beneficial. The new boss implemented a quota system, mandated less personal contact between the clinical professionals and their clients, and insisted on stricter controls and more paperwork. Since Dana's primary focus was on helping her clients, the added bureaucracy pushed her to the point of quitting. "I think my boss took his leadership secrets from Atilla the Hun," she complained to her husband. "I don't believe there's a sensitive bone in his body."

Within the influential or popular personality—the otter—lies a strong drive for acceptance and affirmation and a desire to express thoughts and opinions verbally. Frequently such individuals tend to operate as "mavericks" and test whatever limits they have been given. Relationships are more important to them than goals, and they have an intense need to have fun, to be with people, and to feel the freedom to express themselves. Florence Littauer gives a clever description of those, including herself, who fit this personality type: "They can speak anytime, on any subject, with or without information."

For the Cindy in our discussion group, talking with her customers wasn't just a way to ensure a good tip; it also fulfilled her need to be around people and to get laughs. When her boss sarcastically suggested one day that if she wanted to continue exchanging jokes with the clients she could find a job with the local comedy club, Cindy felt intensely frustrated. "After all," she complained, "that's my strength—relating to people, making them feel glad they came in. Nobody is as well liked by the customers as I am. He just doesn't understand how important that is in getting them to come back."

GETTING ALONG WITH THE BOSS

Perhaps the one area where personality differences create the most chaos is with the boss. According to author Julie Lopez, three-fourths of all the managerial staff she surveyed had trouble with their superiors.[8] They felt their bosses didn't understand them and that they all had personality problems. Lopez divides bosses into four categories that showed a remarkable similarity to the four major personality types.[9]

Her first category, *the incompetent boss,* talks on the phone all day and doesn't know how to get things done. Lopez suggests that employees of this type help the boss do her work and work at making her look good.

Her second category, *the workaholic boss,* resembles the powerful lion. This kind of boss often treats employees like slaves and expects everyone to work the same kind of incredible hours he does. Do it the boss's way, Lopez suggests, but don't let yourself be bullied into unreasonable demands.

The phantom boss, similar to the steady, perfectionistic beaver, likes to stay out of the action and communicate by detailed, written memos. Lopez's answer for getting along with this kind of boss is to communicate back in writing, making sure to enumerate all your accomplishments.

Her fourth category, *the wimp*, resembles the peaceful, compliant golden retriever. This is the boss "who can't take charge, tries to avoid conflict, and becomes paralyzed when faced with a decision." Her solution is to boost his confidence, while feeding him information he can use to make decisions.

LOVING OUR NEIGHBORS AT WORK

Scripture instructs us to love our neighbors as ourselves, and, since our neighbors include those we work with—our bosses, our fellow workers, and our clients—it is important that we get to know them and understand how to relate to them in a manner consistent with their own best interests. After all, that's what loving a person is all about. Remember, we aren't simply seeking harmony for the sake of harmony.

That's why it is important that we follow the apostle Paul's instructions in 1 Thessalonians 5:14 for getting along with others. The verb "comfort" in verse 14 basically means to be called alongside to help. Used by Jesus to describe the Holy Spirit in the Upper Room Discourse, it fits perfectly into the workplace scenario, where individuals labor alongside each other and need assistance and encouragement. As he explains the process of encouragement, Paul gives three specific relational techniques, followed by a general principle that applies to all three.

First, the apostle instructs us to warn or rebuke those who get out of line. The loving thing to do when people do wrong is to confront them. The apostle followed this approach with some in the church in Thessalonica who had chosen to be idle and refused to continue working (2 Thessalonians 3:10–11). Labeling them "busybodies," he pointed out that the rule should be "No work, no eat."

The apostle's second axiom for getting along is to cheer up those who are at the point of giving up. When people reach the end of their ropes, when they desperately need help or assistance, the thing to do is *not* to confront or brow-beat them. Instead, that's the time to provide them with cheer and encouragement. When Paul was sailing toward Rome and his ship was about to be wrecked, he didn't give his ship-mates the second stanza of the "I told you so" song. Instead, he cheered them up by saying, "We'll lose the ship, but God has assured me there will be no loss of life. Hang in there!"

Paul's third axiom for getting along is to support the weak. The Greek word he uses for "uphold" in 1 Thessaloni-ans 5:14, *antechomai*, includes the letter *chi*—the counter-part to the English letter "x." In a sense, it's as though the Holy Spirit led Paul to this word to provide a picture of the strongest possible support we find in any kind of building or bridge—a cross-brace, which is what "x" resembles. It is both our privilege and our responsibility to provide the kind of support individuals need to succeed in what they are do-ing. If we support those with weaknesses, we all gain strength, since no chain is stronger than its weakest link.

Paul's final general imperative in this verse, "Be patient with all," has great significance for the workplace environ-ment. The verb he uses carries the idea of suffering a long time under heat and pressure. Working with people will pro-duce pressure, and heat will be generated on occasion. If we follow Paul's instructions for maintaining relationships, we can minimize the stresses of the workplace.

THE WORKAHOLIC

In an earlier book, several colleagues and I identified a number of personality hazards of the burnout-prone "obses-sive-compulsive" personality.[10] Although the term *obsessive-compulsive* is often used of a clinical disorder, having an obsessive-compulsive personality indicates that we think of things over and over again (obsessions), while experiencing feelings that drive us to act on those thoughts (compulsions). Obsessive-compulsive behavior can lead to positive results—for example, the successful head football coach who watches the previous week's game film twenty times, or the salesman who makes extensive client lists, complete with data about each one, carefully indexed and filed. Obsessives try to be right on time for appointments and make extensive "to do" lists, often attempting to do two or more things at once. They tend to be extremely time and money conscious.

In our research on obsessive-compulsives we discovered two primary types—the qualitative and the quantitative. The *qualitative* tends toward perfectionism and may result from a blend of perfectionistic and peaceful types. They typically take a long time to get things done and want to redo anything that isn't exactly right. They typically focus on one project to the exclusion of everything else. If your secretary is a qualitative perfectionist and you assign her two additional tasks while she's still in the middle of completing the one thing you asked her to do earlier, she may feel a high level of stress. If, on the other hand, she has more of the quantitative obsessive-compulsive traits, she may welcome the challenge, saying, "No problem, boss. Anything else you'd like me to do?" In fact, she may feel bored if you have only one project for her.

A *quantitative* obsessive is typically more "type A" and tends to be a combination of the powerful and popular or perfectionist and popular—an unusual combination, but not impossible. The quantitative perfectionist gives himself twenty things to do in a day, completes seventeen, then wants to kick himself that evening for not getting the other three tasks done. His motivation is likely to be to please or win approval from others. His weakness is that he may not concentrate on doing as thorough a job as he is capable of.

The *qualitative* perfectionist, on the other hand, tends to work more slowly, struggle to get one thing done perfectly, and have trouble deciding what is absolutely perfect. Hence, she never considers a project completed—after all, there may still be some way it could be improved. While the quantitative obsessive rushes headlong from activity to activity, the qualitative obsessive methodically perfects each detail of every task. The problem is, neither is able to achieve a balance of strategic time focus or a way of approaching things.

Many individuals from either category can be accurately labeled *workaholics*. Unfortunately, today's workplace often seems crowded with individuals who are literally addicted to work. There is a difference between working hard, or even working long hours, and being a workaholic. Many who choose to work long hours are capable of setting aside their work. But from the workaholic's perspective, the job is never done, and one should never set it aside until it is done. The workaholic has adopted a behavior pattern similar to the alcoholic, who cannot quit his alcohol consumption even though it is ruining his life. The workaholic *cannot* stop putting his work first—ahead of relationships, personal health, spirituality—even though his work may be killing him or, at the least, undermining the quality of his life. If you are a workaholic, your workplace stress will likely be compounded as you are prone to interact in more intense fashion with other workaholics who also feel driven about their work.

The Old Testament presents a vivid picture of what happens when an individual carries this workaholic pattern to an extreme. Solomon provides a first-person description:

> *Therefore I hated life because the work that was done under the sun was grievous to me, for all is vanity and grasping for the wind. . . . Therefore I turned my heart and despaired of all the labor in which I had toiled under the sun. . . . For what has man for all his labor, and for the striving of his heart with which he has toiled under the sun? For all his days are sorrowful, and his work grievous; even in the night his heart takes no rest. This also is vanity.* (Ecclesiastes 2:17, 20, 22–23)

Solomon's description highlights three characteristics of the life of the individual who has become trapped in an inordinate focus on or an addiction to work. First, life becomes drudgery, a meaningless chasing after the wind. Second, life becomes negative, filled with cynicism and discouragement. Third, life is futile. There seems to be no reward, no real benefit—just the endless cycle of labor and responsibilities, sapped of joy, strength, and meaning.

Later in Ecclesiastes, Solomon presents the alternative: "There is nothing better for a man than that he should eat and drink, and that his soul should enjoy good in his labor. This also, I saw, was from the hand of God. . . . To everything there is a season, a time for every purpose under heaven" (Ecclesiastes 2:24; 3:1). In essence, the king was saying that there is a place for hard work and for enjoying the fruit of labor. Such balance between work and rest is based on the divinely ordained principle that life is seasonal.

The workaholic can often be spotted by telltale signs: a frantic schedule, a tendency to talk primarily about work and responsibility, an inability to say no, and impending cardiac or other health problems. The workaholic's primary focus always seems to be on performance, on getting the job done.

If you have recognized yourself in the profile of the workaholic or from the "Stress Test" on page 143, your first step should be to gain insight into your own hidden agenda. As Jesus explained in John 8:32, the truth is ultimately what sets us free. Understanding why you feel driven to perform and succeed—whether as a perfectionist or a type A—is crucial to regaining balance. Second, you must face the harmful effects of workaholism—on yourself, on your important relationships with people, even on your relationship with God. Third, seeking counsel, gaining insight, and submitting to accountability can play an extremely important role in overcoming the harmful effects of workaholism. Fourth, a long-term plan to work toward balance is more effective than attempting a total or radical personality shift. Just as with the alcoholic, the workaholic tendency may always be present, the temptation toward drivenness never far away. However, the fruit of the Spirit includes self-control (Galatians 5:23), and this fruit can be cultivated through insight, encouragement, and accountability.

 **STRESS TEST** ....

Are You a Workaholic?

To help you identify if you are a workaholic, or how much progress you are making in becoming less of a workaholic, answer the following "true" (T) or "false" (F). The more statements you answer "true," the more of a workaholic you are.

_____ 1. *People who are in authority are no better than I.*

_____ 2. *Once I start a job, I have no peace until I finish it.*

_____ 3. *I like to tell people exactly what I think.*

_____ 4. *I worry a lot about business and financial matters.*

_____ 5. *I often find it difficult to sleep because thoughts about work bother me.*

_____ 6. *At times I cannot sit or lie down because I need to be doing something.*

_____ 7. *My concentration is not what it used to be.*

_____ 8. *I cannot get through a day or a week without a schedule or a list of jobs to do.*

_____ 9. *I believe that the person who works the hardest and longest deserves to get ahead.*

_____ 10. *I frequently feel angry without understanding what or who is bothering me.*

_____ 11. *I always like to be in control and know what is happening around me.*

_____ 12. *I have few or no close friends with whom I share warm feelings openly.*

_____ 13. *I often expect things of myself that no one else would ask.*

_____ 14. *I sometimes worry about whether I've done something wrong or made a mistake.*

_____ 15. *I want others to see me as not having any faults.*

....

PRACTICAL STEPS

The most important thing is to learn to accept yourself. Sadly, some of us have trouble accepting the personality God has given us. We'd far rather be somebody else! However, radical personality shifts are about as rare as brain transplants. God wants us to recognize and strengthen the strengths we possess while working on our weaknesses.

If my personality is a strong, powerful one, I'll want to understand the hazards of seizing control or running roughshod over other people; I will work to develop greater sensitivity toward others. If my personality is like the otter, I may need to redirect some of my people focus and exercise more responsibility to get tasks done. If I am more of a passive, golden retriever type, I may need to increase my personal resolve to get things done. And if mine is the beaverlike perfectionist personality, I may need to lighten up and learn to focus more on people than on the projects at hand.

If my first responsibility in dealing with the stresses of people at work is to better understand my own strengths and weaknesses and achieve insight-based balance in my own life, *the second step is to recognize the value of others who differ from me.* Solomon said in Proverbs 27:17, "As iron sharpens iron, so a man sharpens the countenance of his friend." In other words, there is something I can gain from every other individual, something that can sharpen me so that I will develop in character and become more effective in performance. It may seem as though my overbearing boss, my passive employee, the individual whose personality is on the opposite end of the spectrum from me holds no positive benefit to me. However, even among Jesus' disciples we see how the popular and powerful Peter could benefit from the more perfectionistic and peaceful John, and vice versa.

The third step is to recognize and identify the basic personality types of those we work with. It is, however, important not to go overboard and pigeonhole individuals or say things such as "She'll never get anything done; she's just a peaceful person," or, "I'll never be able to work with him—he'd probably bite my head off." Instead, by recognizing the personality traits we see in others, we can better understand their needs and characteristics and relate more effectively.

Florence Littauer once pointed out on "Life Perspectives" that an obvious way to spot "popular sanguines" is by their brightly colored clothing. Interestingly, Florence had come to the studio wearing what was undoubtedly the most colorful suit I've ever seen! Her husband, Fred, on the other hand—a powerful perfectionist—was dressed impeccably in shades of gray. Florence suggests that you can spot the more popular person by their tendency to speak more loudly than others and to dominate conversations. She says they tend to be more verbal in relationships and casual in their work style.

The powerful individual often moves more rapidly, demonstrates greater intensity and determination to establish his or her point in conversations, and uses strong gestures. Whereas the powerful personality takes a more "no frills" or functional approach, the popular personality likes to have all the frills and decorative combinations at work and in life.

The beaverlike perfectionist likes to have everything neatly organized, with every paper and piece of equipment in perfect order, and all files carefully labeled. They like to keep and frequently update an inventory of all their equipment, usually make it a point to have no more than one project on their desk at a time, and pay careful attention to detail.

The peaceful, easygoing golden retriever personality may tend to blend into the crowd rather than standing out like the rapidly moving, powerful individual or the more talkative popular personality. They seldom seem in a hurry, don't develop a large numbers of friends, but typically have a few people they are very close to. Often people are attracted to them because of their willingness to listen. Their workspace is seldom flashy and usually isn't messy or particularly neat. However, they may have a number of projects that they haven't completed. They find it easier to procrastinate if they run into an obstacle while working on a particular assignment. They tend to like things within easy reach and may allow some clutter to develop in order to make that possible.

Once you have identified the personalities of the people you work with, you can begin to recognize their needs. The more popular otter type needs attention and approval most of all. You will find it much easier to get along with them if you affirm them often, express appreciation, and pay attention to them—even if you sometimes find it difficult or frustrating.

Cindy the waitress was ready to quit her job because the owner of the restaurant where she worked didn't believe in handing out compliments. Cindy was a person of boundless energy and creativity, but her batteries were recharged by attention and approval—and her boss and fellow workers gave her very little of either.

The basic need of the powerful person is for appreciation, since he or she tends to operate more on a performance basis. Since Vern was the head of his company, he found very little appreciation in his workplace. There was one exception to this rule. Phil, his administrative assistant, who was a peaceful, golden retriever type, frequently expressed his gratitude to "the boss" for his help and personal support. He also showed appreciation for Vern's choices, in contrast to Bob, the chief financial officer, who constantly seemed critical of Vern's decisions. It's not surprising that Phil experienced greater job satisfaction—and great job security—as a result of his affirmation and appreciation.

The perfectionistic, beaver-type personality just wants to be understood, since his or her key needs are for understanding, communication, and sensitivity. David was willing to accept the policies of the principal at his school—but he struggled with the fact that his principal didn't take the time to communicate them to him in an orderly fashion or to understand the difficulties they might lead to in a classroom.

The peaceful individual may appear to have no needs at all. But he or she often struggles with self-worth and the need to be respected in order to feel self-respect. Rich, the golden retriever mechanic, often thinks back to the boss he considers the best he ever had—a boss who listened to him, who accepted his suggestions, and who expressed respect for the good job he did.

To recognize the value of others who differ from us and seek to meet their needs is to follow Jesus' mandate to love our neighbor as ourselves.

A fifth suggestion for getting along with others in the workplace involves developing good communication skills. The most fundamental communication principle in Scripture can be found in Ephesians 4:15—"Speak the truth in love." The key to this principle is balance; not just speaking the truth, perhaps in a way that blows others away, but taking a loving approach to communication. In addition, communication should take place on the basis of the four principles we considered from 1 Thessalonians 5:14—confronting when appropriate, cheering up when appropriate, supporting when appropriate, exercising patience at all times.

Sixth, the "wise as serpents, harmless as doves" principle of Matthew 10:16 is essential. When Jesus sent his disciples out into their "workplace," He warned them not to attack —the dove is a bird of peace. Neither were they to place their heads where others could step on them. That, in essence, is the wisdom of the serpent.

The seventh principle involves making it your goal to love your neighbor as yourself by getting along as much as you are able. Romans 12:18 says, "If it is possible, as much as depends on you, live peaceably with all men." Getting along depends on the responses of two individuals, and since we can be responsible only for our own actions, we will never be able to get along with some people. Perhaps we remind them of someone who hurt them deeply in the past— or of themselves. Whatever the case, we are responsible only for what we can do, and we must recognize this limitation while doing all we can to love our workplace neighbor.

Finally, one of the surest ways to relieve stress in the workplace is to choose to forgive those who wrong us. There is much in Scripture on this important principle. Furthermore, bitterness, a primary cause of burnout, is usually the result of refusing to forgive and holding grudges, which are nursed over time, along with a subtle motive to get even or take vengeance. The New Testament is filled with exhortations to forgive and warnings against holding grudges. We are told to always turn vengeance over to God (Romans 12:19–20; 1 Thessalonians 5:15; 1 Peter 3:9).

I have taken an important step toward getting along with others at work when I choose to forgive their actions or habits that irritate me and work at accepting them and demonstrating Christlike love. This is the key to minimizing our personality differences as a cause of stress in the workplace.

CHAPTER NINE

THE PETER PRINCIPLE AND STRESS

N orm was one of the best supply clerks in the factory where he was employed. He was able to get along well with those who worked alongside him. He filled outside orders effectively and obeyed instructions cheerfully and accurately. In short, Norm was a good follower.

Before long Norm was promoted to the position of parts manager. Now, instead of being part of the group, he was "middle management." But Norm wasn't really cut out to have the self-initiative and even the solitude he needed to fill his new post effectively. He still spent a lot of his time hanging around the men in the shop, joking with them, handing out unwanted advice, and interfering with their work performance. He found it difficult to give brief instructions and let people get on with their jobs. His subordinates soon became inefficient and unhappy.

Norm also spent a lot of his time in the general manager's office, probably because of his feelings of insecurity about his new job. If the boss didn't have time to talk with him, he would sit in the outer office exchanging gossip with the boss's secretary. She didn't feel she could tell him to get out, so her work began to suffer too. Norm's boss began investing an increasing amount of time figuring out "make-work" errands, just to keep Norm out of his and his secretary's hair.

Unfortunately, what happened to Norm is in many workplaces the rule rather than the exception. It has been expressed in a principle identified by psychologist and consultant Dr. Laurence J. Peter. The basic premise behind what has come to be called the "Peter Principle" is what he identifies as growing occupational incompetence.

> *Occupational incompetence is everywhere.... We see indecisive politicians posing as resolute statesmen.... Public servants who are indolent and insolent; ... and governors whose innate servility prevents their actually governing. In our sophistication we virtually shrugged aside the immoral cleric, corrupt judge, incoherent attorney, author who cannot write and English teacher who cannot spell.[1]*

In its simplest form, the Peter Principle is based on the observation that "In a hierarchy every employee tends to rise to his level of incompetence."[2] From my observations, many people who have become stressed in their jobs seem to have risen through the hierarchy to a point just beyond their level of skill and competence and become "stuck" in a position where they are neither qualified, competent, nor comfortable. If you find that your job is a major source of frustration and stress, consider whether you have been promoted beyond your own level of competence.

LEVEL OF INCOMPETENCE

When Laurence Peter first presented his idea to the public in a seminar in 1960, the response was "a mixture of hostility and laughter."[3] Eventually Peter shared his conclusions with actor and writer Raymond Hall, and the two collaborated to write what eventually became the book *The Peter Principle*. After fourteen rejection notices over a two-year period, the book ended up defying traditional publishers' wisdom by occupying the number-one position on the nonfiction best-seller list for more than twenty weeks.

I recall thinking when I first read Peter's book, *There's a lot of common sense in his observations.* So when I began to list various causes of workplace stress, the Peter Principle was one of the first things that came to mind.

Editor or Director?

I thought about Phil, who began his career as a successful editor. A skilled writer, Phil had coauthored a number of books and ghostwritten several more, all with appropriate credit. Because he was skilled with words and good with people, Phil soon found himself promoted to editorial director. He told me on several occasions that he found the administrative aspects of his work frustrating, but he enjoyed being involved in the writing and editing process.

Before long, Phil was offered the position of president of a new publishing company. The investors were convinced that he was the man to lead them. After all, he had recognized numerous successful authors and given them their start, and his fingerprints were on several genuine best-sellers. Overlooking his admitted dislike for administrative details or a hard-nosed approach to the bottom line, or the big-picture focus essential for successful CEOs in any realm, the men urged Phil to accept the position, and he did.

He focused his energies on cultivating several authors he liked and working on projects he enjoyed, while allowing more distasteful aspects of his new job to slide. When the issues he had neglected began pressing in on him, Phil found himself suffering from physical problems, including an ulcer, rapid heartbeat, and insomnia. Before long he was fired. To use Laurence Peter's terminology, Phil had risen to his level of incompetence and become stuck there, until he was dislodged by the board of his newly formed company.

Cook or Manager?

The same thing happened to Jane, one of the best cooks I ever met. She has a skill for preparing Cajun food that may equal that of famous chef Paul Prudhomme. She took great delight in getting the freshest of ingredients, taking the time to prepare them correctly, and presenting them in the most tasteful manner. Because of her success as chef for a small seafood restaurant, she was made the manager of the restaurant. Since her first love was cooking, she continued to concentrate her efforts on making sure the restaurant produced the high-quality food she had made it known for.

However, she didn't fare as well in her efforts to control the budget or maintain order and discipline among the staff waiters, hostesses, and buspeople. Her concern for acquiring only the freshest and best ingredients was no longer counterbalanced by a manager's concern for bottom-line costs, since she was now wearing both the chef's and manager's hats.

However, Jane was just successful enough and hard-working enough that her boss was convinced she could manage the entire chain of five restaurants he eventually owned. Her appointment to that position was a disaster waiting to happen. Before long, what had been a smoothly running operation under his oversight became one crisis after another. Jane felt unhappy, since she was no longer able to spend time doing what she enjoyed, and no one else was happy with the results of her "management by crisis" approach.

Because of his loyalty to Jane, the boss insisted on keeping her in place and because of her persistence in not giving up or admitting she had been promoted beyond her competence, she managed to keep her position. Jane, her boss, and virtually every employee of the five restaurants over which she now had supervision were all affected by unwanted and unwarranted stress, much of which was caused by Jane's promotion beyond her skills.

 **STRESS TEST**

Have You Risen to Your Level of Incompetence?

Check the questions you would answer with a yes.

☐ 1. *Do you neglect aspects of your work that you find uninteresting or very difficult?*

☐ 2. *Do you fail to see the importance or necessity of one or more of your job duties?*

☐ 3. *Do you make excuses, to yourself or to others, as to why the same projects remain undone?*

☐ 4. *Do you go out of your way to let your supervisor know what a good worker you are?*

☐ 5. *Have you accepted the credit for a good job done by somebody else?*

☐ 6. *Are you proud of being promoted higher than anyone else with your age, experience, or level of education?*

☐ 7. *Does your spouse often feel that your work is more important to you than he or she is?*

☐ 8. *Are you using fewer of your skills at work than you were five years ago?*

☐ 9. *Do you sometimes wish you were still in that job your last promotion removed you from?*

☐ 10. *When you are offered a promotion, do you think more about the pay raise, perks, and title than about the added responsibilities?*

☐ 11. *Are you regularly dissatisfied with performance reviews because either you cannot accept less than perfection or they are lower than they should be?*

☐ 12. *Do your co-workers or subordinates find it difficult to relate to you on a friendly basis?*

SCORING: If you checked more than half the boxes, you may be rising, or already have risen, above your level of competence.

WORK HIERARCHIES

The word *hierarchy* comes from a combination of two Greek terms and by definition describes "a system with grades of status or authority ranking one above another in a series, or the set of persons in such a system."[4] The concept is said to have originated with priests who were organized into various classes during the Middle Ages, including cardinals, bishops, and ultimately the pope.

During the feudal era there was little if any parallel between the religious hierarchy and employment. According to Laurence Peter, "In feudal times a man was content to live within a nonpromotion system and remain at a level of competence for a lifetime."[5] He defined competence from the perspective of both an input and output. Input competence involves "contributing to the smooth internal functioning of the organization." Output competence is "the performance of a job in a way which produces the desired output."[6]

From feudal times until just a few decades ago, a high percentage of people chose the same vocations their fathers and uncles had held. Second-, third-, and fourth-generation farmers continued to till the land. A man whose father had been an electrician, a mechanic, or a painter would learn that trade from his father and wind up doing it himself.

My wife's father was a skilled painter and painting contractor who always worked just enough men to get the job done. He demonstrated enough pride in his work and wisdom in his approach to never grow beyond his ability to oversee the quality, and he avoided the major administrative headaches some of his friends found when they attempted to "grow their business" to the level of a major paint contracting operation. My wife's brother and our brother-in-law both learned painting, drywall finishing, and wallpaper hanging from Kathy's dad and have used that skill to earn a living.

My own father spent more than forty years working for the railroad, first as a fireman shoveling coal on steam engines, then as an engineer or "hoghead" as they were often called. The hours were long and the work sometimes stressful, but Dad never expressed any desire to be promoted to road foreman of engines, trainmaster, vice president, or CEO of the Southern Railway System, as it was then named. My brother John followed in my father's footsteps and is now a conductor on the same railroad. He has no ambition to become an officer of the Norfolk Southern.

In my father-in-law's painting operation there were basically two or three levels of hierarchy. He gave the orders, and the men who worked for him took them. As a painting subcontractor, my father-in-law was subject to the general contractors who hired him for new construction or to clients who employed his services to refurbish existing homes. Construction schedules had to be met and adjustments made for carpet layers, electricians, plumbers, even roofers.

PETER AND MURPHY

Mitch gained his start working for a small-operation painting contractor like my father-in-law. However, he had plans to climb the ladder of success. His goal was to become the largest general contractor in his hometown.

A hard worker and a quick study, Mitch became a skilled painter. He was also extremely goals oriented—he knew where he was headed and had a good idea of what it would take to get there. He thoroughly enjoyed the creativity and attention to detail involved in painting or hanging beautifully flocked wallpaper. He took great pride in doing a good job. But he also wanted to make a lot of money so that he could support his wife and family in a big way. Plus, Mitch coveted the prestige of being recognized as a leader in his chosen field. So he continued pushing his way to the top.

After becoming a large painting contractor, Mitch began building houses as a general contractor. But he found it much more stressful than his previous work as a subcontractor, when he dealt only with the painting. Mitch continued to enjoy his work, and although he wasn't quite as good or effective as he had been, people still considered him to be "on-track" to success.

Then Mitch landed his first big contract—to build a major apartment complex in a different city. He would have to live apart from his family for several months, take his crew along, fit into a new system of building codes, and establish new relationships for purchasing materials. Another factor he would soon learn about was the strength of the labor unions in the city where he would be overseeing construction of what was to be his crowning achievement in his rise to contracting success. It turned out to be a monumental disaster.

We have been talking about the Peter Principle, but this may be a good time to review another maxim—Murphy's Law. It contains three main components: One, nothing is as easy as it looks; two, everything takes longer and costs more than you think; three, if anything can go wrong, it will.[7]

To hear Mitch tell it in retrospect, when it came to his major project, Murphy "was an optimist." For one thing, Mitch and the men who came with him to work on the apartment megaproject felt the stress of being away from their families. Then Mitch discovered that, although he thought he had done his homework, material prices were running 10 to 15 percent higher than he had anticipated when he bid the job. So he stood a real chance of losing money.

But the straw that broke the camel's back was the conflict with union officials in the city where he was working. "I never realized just how stressful dealing with labor unions could be," he told me later. "I always assumed, if you just treated your men fairly, you could expect an honest day's work, union or not. Boy, did I learn the hard way!"

Today Mitch still works on large apartment complexes. He isn't the general contractor; he just subs the painting and wallpaper work. Instead of a large crew, he has only himself, his son, and three other men. But he's much happier. As he puts it, "I may have taken a few steps back down the ladder.

But I'm still alive and in my right mind. Plus I have time for my family, for church, and to get involved in the lives of other people. Those things are more important than making a lot of money or being successful. "The climb to the top really isn't what it's cracked up to be."

Many years ago during my seminary days I heard Howard Hendricks present a graphic description of the "man who climbed the ladder of success only to discover it was leaning against the wrong building." I have talked to many people who made that same sad discovery.

One summer afternoon my wife and I sat on the patio behind our home with Jane. "When I started operating that first little seafood restaurant," Jane said, "I ran the whole thing myself. I opened up at noon. Closed up at night. I bought the fish from a supplier I trusted, a man I knew who trucked crawfish in from Henderson, Louisiana. Another man brought in shrimp. We didn't charge a lot for our food, the atmosphere wasn't all that great. But the place was clean and comfortable. Our food was top quality and the people who came in regarded me as a friend."

Jane was in charge of the business and felt confident in making decisions based on her judgment and experience. She felt the joy of accomplishment and was satisfied doing what she did well. Then her boss came to Jane with a proposition. A Chinese restaurant on the other side of town was going out of business. Sam intended to buy the restaurant, and he wanted Jane to run both restaurants.

"I tried overseeing the original restaurant at noon and the new location in the evening. So I made rules to run things. I gave the staff rules for purchasing food, but I was unable to keep in personal contact with our best suppliers. Our costs went up and, since I was unable to be involved the way I had been, the quality went down."

Before long Sam had purchased three more restaurants and put Jane in charge of them as well. Now she wound up spending most of her time in an office. Gradually she began to realize she had lost the pleasures of her job, and she was no longer particularly effective. "I was almost never able to be in the kitchen or do any direct supervision of the people. More problems kept cropping up, and I kept making rules to cover them. I became a bureaucrat, and I felt miserable."

When I explained to Jane the Peter Principle, she nodded vigorously. "It fits me to a tee. That's exactly what happened. I wound up doing less and less of what I was good at and more and more of what I couldn't handle. Don, I can't tell you how stressful it became!"

Today Jane is out of the restaurant business. Instead, she has been hired as a cook and household manager for a wealthy family. She enjoys what she does, and the hierarchy is simple. The family gives her general instructions and a great deal of freedom. She prepares healthy meals and oversees two other household staffers. "It's almost like I've died and gone to heaven," she says with a smile.

CLIMBING THE LADDER

Hierarchies in themselves aren't wrong. Scripture establishes the validity of hierarchies in passages like Romans 13:1, where Paul urges respect and submission to the "governing authorities." The apostle points to both the threat of punishment and the demand of good conscience (v. 5) as reasons to submit to authority. Hierarchies have also been established in God's economy for the home (Colossians 3:18–21) and the workplace—even including the master/slave relationship of the first century (3:22–4:1).

However, another factor explains why the Peter Principle often generates stress. Not only do hierarchies exist, but the natural response of people seems to be to push toward the top. Think about the last time you attended a popular play at the theater, a major sporting event, or a musical concert. You probably gathered with a large crowd of others outside the gates, waiting with varying degrees of patience. Finally, someone came to open the gates, and the crowd began pushing its way inside. If seating had not been preassigned, most people rushed as rapidly as possible to get to the best seats. That's just a small example of what Jesus pointed out in the lives of the religious leaders of His day, the scribes and Pharisees: "They love the best places at feasts, the best seats in the synagogues, greetings in the marketplaces, and to be called by men 'Rabbi, rabbi'" (Matthew 23:6–7). It's that innate human desire to climb the ladder just as high as we can to gain as much fame, recognition, or fortune as possible.

It was a game the apostle Paul had learned to play well when he was Saul the Pharisee. As he explained in his letter to the Philippians, he considered himself in no way inferior to any top-ranking Pharisee (3:4–6). It was not until he made Jesus Christ the focus of his life and ambition that he learned to take those things he had previously counted gain and consider them loss for Christ (3:7–8).

Believers can fall into the trap of making personal ambition a priority; they can fall in love with the world and its methods (1 John 2:15). The apostle John identified three major sources of temptation that are part of the world's way—the lust of the flesh, the lust of the eyes, and the pride of life (v. 16). The first involves the desire to have what brings pleasure and enjoyment—sex, food, and so on. The lust of the eyes involves the drive to possess in its most basic form. It's often called materialism. The third factor is what John calls the pride of life.

The word *alazon*, translated "pride," comes from the root of a word that means to wander about the country. It was used of a vagabond and describes someone who is "on the move."[8] The term was used twice by Paul: once in a list of negative values associated with sin and the Fall (Romans 1:30), the other time to warn his protégé Timothy of the danger of the last days (2 Timothy 3:2). The term came to describe an arrogant boasting or those who present themselves as something they are not. John's use of the word seems to describe those who are trying to become what they aren't or to "move up" in life.

We see evidences of this on every hand today—turf wars in work and ministry, bureaucratic escalation in government, power struggles all over. There's just a natural temptation to want to move ahead and take control. The problem is, how are we to distinguish this sinful drive from the desire for excellence or the drive to move beyond mediocrity? Sometimes the differences are subtle.

BIBLICAL DEFICIENCY

But we must move beyond the theories of Laurence Peter, just as we did 'with Stephen Covey and other management gurus. Their analysis of the problem is accurate up to a point, yet they fail to provide a thoroughly biblical explanation for the problems they identify or recognize God's solutions. Peter's concept of "hierarchical regression" does show "the quality of life declining and viable social institutions degenerating into giant, ineffective, self-perpetuating bureaucracies. Everything from products to presidents become less interesting and mediocrity triumphs as the hierarchy eradicates excellence."[9] The problem is there for all to see.

However, identifying the effects of sin is one thing; applying the biblical solution is another. To suggest that man can somehow fulfill his destiny apart from a proper connection with his Creator is to minimize the devastating effects of the Fall.

Peter laments what he calls the "processionary puppet" who goes through the motions of life—filling in forms, carrying out meaningless rituals, striving to maintain the status quo, and seeking promotions to move up the "follow the leader" ladder. The biblical explanation for what Peter has observed is that "we have each gone our own way" as the prophet Isaiah pointed out centuries ago. Every human has been stained by the effects of sin. No matter how hard we try to lift ourselves up, the impact of the Fall drives each of us beyond incompetence to failure.

WISDOM NEEDED

For the Christian, God's provision of wisdom and counsel for making good decisions becomes essential. There are principles that can help us choose to step off the "treadmill of success" and find meaning and contentment in life.

Joe and the Peter Principle

Joe was an excellent car salesman. He loved what he did. He was gifted at talking with people but despised paperwork. He made a good living selling cars, and he had learned to depend on the secretarial team at the dealership to help him handle the paperwork.

On three different occasions Joe's boss pushed him to accept the position of sales manager, telling him, "You'll be good at it, just like you have been with selling. Paperwork is a piece of cake; anybody can handle it. You're a natural leader. We need leaders. It's the loyal thing to do for the company. We need you to take this position."

The boss even enlisted the owner of the dealership to try to persuade the young salesman. Joe carefully considered the opportunity for increased income, the recognition, the corner office, the prestigious new title on his business card. Because he was a Christian, he committed his decision to the Lord, since he believed that the promise in James 1:5—if anyone asked for wisdom, God would give it—applied to him and specifically to this situation.

Joe also was convinced of the value of the multitude of counselors. For more than a year he had been part of a small group of men who met regularly for breakfast at a nearby restaurant to encourage each other and hold each other accountable. Joe shared his concerns about the job offer with those men and with Ken, his pastor. Ken encouraged Joe to study three verses in Proverbs that referred to a "multitude of counselors." He explained how individuals, churches, and even governments need direction: "Where there is no counsel, the people fall" (Proverbs 11:14). He advised Joe, "There's a lot to be said for the safety afforded by a multitude of counselors. After all, think about how often doctors encourage you to get a second opinion."

From Proverbs 15:22 Ken pointed out that without counsel, purposes are frustrated, "but in the multitude of counselors they are established." "Think about your goals, Joe," he urged. "What's really important to you? Is it the carrot they're holding out to attract you to this new position? Think about the impact on the time you'll have left to spend with your wife and your family. Would you still be able to meet with your accountability group? How do you think you would feel a year or two after taking this new position? Will your purposes be frustrated or established?"

Finally, Joe and pastor Ken looked at Proverbs 20:4–5, which talks about the inevitable conflicts of life. Ken pointed out the previous verse, "which talks about strengthening your strengths, using them to the max." He suggested that Joe might be at risk of falling into the Peter Principle and violating Proverbs 24:5. "Instead of strengthening your strengths, you may actually wind up minimizing your strengths and maximizing your weaknesses. That will lead to conflicts. Now, when Proverbs talks about waging war, there's more involved than just serving in the military or fighting massive battles. There are wars in the boardroom, battles on the management teams, conflict all through life.

"I'd recommend that you try to determine which option will likely lead to more conflict and which will produce less. Then ask yourself, *If I accept this position, will it leave me with enough margin in my life to handle the demands on my health, time demands, and other factors?*

Joe prayed about the decision, continued to seek the counsel of his pastor and his accountability group, and even talked to a friend who had accepted a similar promotion at a dealership across town. "If I had to do it over again," the manager told him, "I would have stuck with selling cars. You wouldn't believe the headaches, the grief. Sure, I bring home more money. I bought a boat and a set of golf clubs and don't have time to enjoy them. I feel like a stranger to my kids, and my wife and I are having more conflict than we've ever experienced. I'd like to find a way out of the rat race."

It didn't take long for Joe to make up his mind. He already had a satisfying life. He just needed to fine-tune some things. He would have more time to enjoy and value his family if he stayed with his sales job. Providing his family more money wasn't as important as being available himself. Furthermore, his personal well-being was important, not to mention his peace of mind. Joe became convinced that the seduction of more money and prestige were just that—an empty seduction, one he shouldn't respond to.

"I spent some time reading the book of Ecclesiastes," he later told Ken. "I was amazed at all the pursuits Solomon tried and how he found them all vanity. I thought about a verse I came across—Proverbs 13:11: 'Wealth gotten by vanity shall be diminished, but he that gathers by labor shall increase.' I decided that a simple, hardworking approach to my present responsibility was better than trying to climb the ladder of success." Joe provides us with a classic example of how to deal biblically with the Peter Principle.

Management as Ministry

I'm not saying that only people with sinful and selfish motives "climb the ladder" to management. Not at all. Some people work in businesses they really enjoy and understand, develop leadership skills as they move into management, and keep their priorities in balance while leading in a humble yet effective manner. Some Christians have found incredible ministry opportunities on the job when they become known as bosses who are good at what they do.

Barb is a good example. Although not officially a manager at McDonald's, she trained new employees, and her seven or eight years of experience in a job with a three-month turnover rate made her the "resident expert." More important, she was known as a Christian with a gentle, loving spirit. In a job staffed mostly by teenagers, forty-year-old Barb was in a position to be an example, a good listener, and a wise counselor.

Carol found her job as editor of her college yearbook to be a demanding, time-consuming undertaking. Yet she enjoyed the job experience, the team spirit developed in the office, and the satisfaction of a good final product—and she found an unexpected side benefit: She was able to use her spiritual gift of encouragement to bring out the best in people and affirm quality work. "One of the staff members had a tendency to sulk after I'd said no to one of her ideas," Carol says as an example. "I went to her more than once and said, 'Look, if it's that important to you, don't take my no as final. Fight me on it by giving me some good reasons, and I just might reconsider.' I had another employee who was very strong and knew exactly what he wanted. I took the opposite approach to him, because he needed to know how to accept the word *no*: I carefully considered his impassioned arguments, and I told him yes when I could. But if I couldn't, I told him no, and I let him know that 'no' was final. Seeing these two individuals develop their strengths over the course of a year, and knowing I had had a small part in it, was one of the most satisfying experiences I've ever had."

Chris finds that being a fair employer gives him opportunities to witness to those under him. Michael has learned that his reputation as a Christian—and a compassionate boss—has become known even in other stores in the chain where he manages a drugstore. And Thomas, though he admits he has a hard time telling others he is a Christian, knows that his employees value his leadership and his expertise while he works on becoming a bolder witness.

How can you know when it's right to seek or accept a management position? Should you move up the ladder if given a chance? Double-check your motives. Is this a power issue, or do you really want to lead by being a servant? Talk with those to whom you are accountable about your motives and the time commitment involved, and discuss and pray over the idea with your family. Search for God's guidance. And don't say yes before you are certain that the move is what God would want for you.

Practical Suggestions

Here are some practical insights that can help you avoid winding up in a frustrating position of incompetency.

First, whatever you do, *always begin by seeking God's direction.* Granted, there are moral and nonmoral decisions in the world of employment. Certain jobs are wrong in and of themselves, and some promotions may be as well. Sometimes we may be asked to do things in a new, higher position that will violate our conscience.

But even in decisions where the issues are not moral, God wants to walk with us through the decision-making process. As James the apostle explained, if anyone lacks wisdom, he needs to ask of God (James 1:5). The prophet Daniel, when faced with a series of incredibly stressful career choices, sought wisdom from the God of heaven (Daniel 2:10; 6:10; 9:2–4). No wonder he outlasted the entire Babylonian empire and ended his career working for King Cyrus of Persia.

Daniel serves as an example of a man who succeeded in his work because of his commitment to the Scriptures. As he studied Jeremiah's writings, he discovered that God had promised to restore Israel to her land after seventy years, and he based both his prayer and his personal work strategy on what he had learned in Scripture. We too should seek God's will in prayer and examine His Word for general principles that we can apply to our work situations today.

Paul spells out three additional principles in 1 Corinthians 8. First, don't let your freedom become a stumbling block to others (1 Corinthians 8:9). Second, even things that are legal to do may not be profitable or edifying (1 Corinthians 10:23). Third, whatever I put my energies into should be done for God's glory (1 Corinthians 10:31). In every decision I face I can ask myself questions based on these principles. Will the course of action I'm considering help me or hurt me? Will it help or hurt those I am closest to: my spouse and my children? Will it strengthen my relationship with the Lord or hinder my walk with the Lord and my relationships with people?

In addition to seeking wisdom from God through prayer and His Word, *I also need to consider the value of wise counselors.* Every time I have faced a major vocational decision, I have sought the wisdom of a wide range of people whose walk with the Lord I respected. After all, none of us knows everything—we all have blind spots. We may be overlooking some biblical principle, or perhaps we simply have not had the experience others have had to be able to evaluate a certain situation.

Finally, *use common sense.* During my seminary years, W. A. Criswell, who pastored First Baptist Church in Dallas for almost half a century, once pointed out in chapel, "Men, God gave you the five usual senses, but he also gave you two you may not be using—common and horse!" I've often recalled Dr. Criswell's advice when facing decisions where a common-sense approach gave me a straightforward answer to what seemed to be a complex problem. Jesus once reminded His listeners that it is unwise to try to build a building or wage warfare if you can't afford it (Luke 14:28). This "counting the cost" approach has helped me make a number of decisions—vocational and otherwise.

Look for Contentment

What if you are already in a position where you're feeling the frustration of having reached your "level of incompetence"? Is it possible to step out of the rat race? The answer is yes. The key is to look for that important quality described by the apostle Paul in Philippians 4 when he explained, "for I have learned in whatever state I am, to be content" (Philippians 4:11). As he wrote to thank the Philippians for a gift they had sent him, Paul wanted them to know that having more or fewer possessions wasn't the issue with him. He had learned the secret of how to live independently of circumstances! You can do all things, he explained, and handle all situations, through Christ's inner strength (v. 13). Whether his stomach or his bank account was full or empty wasn't the major issue for Paul. Contentment was what mattered.

Later in his ministry, the apostle expanded on this theme as he wrote to Timothy. He urged his protégé to warn masters to demonstrate respect to their slaves in order to glorify God (1 Timothy 6:1). Here are implications for those who feel driven to climb over others to reach "the top" today. Then he shared his personal formula for life: "Godliness with contentment is great gain" (v. 6). From Paul's perspective, material gain was not an automatic sign of godliness or blessing. Many in our day need to be reminded of this. A strong resolve to be rich will likely lead to serious and painful consequences (vv. 8–9). From this Paul drew the principle that "the love of money is a root of all kinds of evil" (v. 10). His point is not that being rich in itself is wrong (v. 17). Rather, those who have been blessed with wealth are to avoid arrogance or dependence on their riches, stay close to the Lord, develop generosity, and focus on laying up eternal rather than temporal treasures (vv. 17–19). The concept of contentment is Scripture's ultimate answer to the Peter Principle.

May God give us the courage to evaluate our lives, determine our true priorities, and replace the Peter Principle with the one Paul wrote—the principle of contentment.

PART THREE

SOLUTIONS TO STRESS
IN THE WORKPLACE

CHAPTER TEN

YOUR WORK
AND GOD

S ome time ago I received an advertising flyer in our interoffice mail. Wanda, one of our directors, had sent it along to me, after adding an interesting editorial comment. According to the ad, simply attending this seminar would help me deal with the greatest single source of stress in my life, identify my stress limits, and overcome frustration, boredom, and role overload. I would learn to stop bringing work-related problems home with me, cultivate a healthy balance between work and home, and identify and deal with my stress triggers.

Turning to the last page, I read, "The seminar starts at precisely 8:45 A.M. and finishes at 4:00 P.M. on the dot." Under it, in Wanda's carefully formed handwriting, was her response: "This one imperative eliminates any credibility your company may have in helping any of our staff deal with stress and/or perfectionistic tendencies." Wanda had concluded that the perfectionistic drivenness of those who presented the seminar—indicated by their tightly structured time limitations— probably meant that they still struggled with the subject for which they claimed to have so many solutions.

As I sat at my desk chuckling and nodding agreement, I couldn't help thinking that in one sense Wanda's point applies to us all. Whether we're talking about workplace stress or any other problem, none of us has reached full resolution. Even the apostle Paul recognized his need to continue to press toward the mark for the prize of the upward calling in Christ Jesus and suggested that anyone who happens to be otherwise minded—in other words, anyone who thinks he has actually arrived—needs to reevaluate his thinking.

However, this certainly doesn't eliminate the possibility of our learning from those who struggle. I agree with something I heard a speaker say in a Spiritual Life Conference many years ago. The direction in which you are moving is of far more importance than the degree to which you have completed your journey. Or, as a friend once put it, the fact that you are headed in the right direction down the right road is more important than the speed at which you are moving.

In chapter 7 we suggested that many of our stresses originate in the conflict between what is urgent and what is important. In other words, we struggle with priorities.

DEFINING PRIORITY

Christians generally agree that God should be the ultimate priority in our lives. Just get permission from your pastor and pass out a simple, two- or three-question survey next Sunday at church. Probably most of those in attendance would give an affirmative answer to such questions as these: Should God be the most important person in your life? Should your spiritual life take precedence over your work?

The problem isn't in reaching agreement on this basic principle. The real issue comes down to two major applicational concerns. The first is, how do we apply the principle? Second, how do we bridge the gap between the principle we agree to and the level at which we practice it?

Some time ago a high school student from Massachusetts wrote to columnist Marilyn vos Savant to ask, "What is virtue? This is the question Socrates posed and the primary question my Western Civilization class is attempting to answer."[1] Now,

Marilyn vos Savant is listed in the Guinness Book of Records as having the highest I.Q. among living humans. She responded, "I find human virtue in the active quest for justice in this world. This would include rewarding goodness wherever it exists, paying no special attention to most things and punishing truly harmful behavior."[2]

The core issue behind this teenager's question is one of authority. Who is qualified to define what virtue or justice really is? Is intelligence the criteria? If so, then vos Savant would be a good person to ask. Yet as the student had learned, a variety of answers has been given to the question Socrates raised. St. Augustine regarded virtue as rejecting the temptations of the flesh, while Sophocles considered it to be obedience to the gods. Voltaire believed that reason lay at the heart of virtue. Is virtue a philosophical or intellectual problem, or is it a religious question?

CHRISTIAN VIRTUE

From a Christian perspective, the ultimate in virtue is that which most clearly reflects the glory or character of God. Given the fact that sin is contrary to the character of God, and since sin is the ultimate source of workplace stress, it seems logical to conclude that the best and most basic antidote for workplace stress is maximum development of godly charac ter in work and in every other area of life. Of course, that's somewhat simplistic; some jobs are more stressful than others by the nature of the work itself. But one thing is clear: A person with the proper perspective on this issue should handle workplace stress better than someone who does not.

However, people take many different views as to how to make God a priority at work. We might arrange these along a line or view them on a spectrum. At one end we would place those who think that the only way to make God a priority is to withdraw from the world as a whole—perhaps enter a monastery or convent, or at least become involved in some distinctively Christian work, such as missions or the pastorate.

At the other end are those who are convinced that Christians should become militant activists about faith at work even to the point of becoming confrontational. A third viewpoint is that Christians have been called to be salt and light, to demonstrate God's character by word and deed. To the degree that such godly character and conduct minimizes workplace stress, those who hold this view—I'm among them—will be helping solve the problem of stress in the workplace, for having purpose and godly goals can help an employee focus and maintain priorities even in difficult places.

As we consider this subject of virtue, it is interesting to note that the Greek word *aretē* can actually mean both excellence and virtue.[3] For the ancient Greeks, *aretē* elevated the focus of man from just earning a living or understanding his environment to the point where he could "lead his life as to attain . . . all of what is . . . highest in human nature."[4] According to the author of *Christian Excellence,* Jon Johnston, biblical writers, guided by God's Spirit, added new dimensions to this Greek concept. He suggests that biblical *aretē*, or excellence, describes "glorifying God, being servants, seeing things in light of the resurrection, having integrity, and being holistic and wholesome in attitude."[5]

It's the kind of thing Paul had in mind when he talked about the "more excellent way," the way of love (1 Corinthians 12:31; 13:1–3), even though he used a different Greek word. Scripture presents God's nature, reflected by His name, as the ultimate source of excellence (Psalm 8:1). When you connect Paul's words about excellence in 1 Corinthians 12:31 with Jesus' mandate to love God with all your heart and to love your neighbor as yourself (Mark 12:28–30), the picture of how we are to establish the priorities in life and work that move us toward excellence begin to come into focus. Jerry Bridges summarizes it this way: "Christian excellence is the quality of life that results when a Christian seeks to live out every area of his life with the aim of pleasing . . . and glorifying God. He is worthy of our most diligent efforts."[6]

WHAT SCRIPTURE SAYS

I'm convinced that I must find the ultimate way to excellence in Scripture. I cannot rely on the principles of human excellence espoused by Peters and Waterman or the "true north principles" based on human conscience advocated by Covey. The apostle Peter wrote that God "has given to us all things that pertain to life and godliness, through the knowledge of Him who called us by glory and virtue" (2 Peter 1:3). Ultimately, virtue develops out of those things I learn in my relationship with God. Paul reminded Timothy that "all Scripture is given by inspiration of God, and is profitable for doctrine, for reproof, for correction, for instruction in righteousness" (2 Timothy 3:16). In other words, His Word provides my ultimate guide for living.

If we are to base prioritizing on a biblical foundation, we must first understand what Scripture teaches about priorities. The Bible uses a wealth of words translated "first" or "one." There are at least eleven terms in the Old Testament and eight in the New.[7] Although many of these words convey chronology, others are used in ways loaded with significance for believers who want to establish priorities.

Jesus used the word *prōtos* to urge His listeners to make the kingdom and righteousness of God the priority in everything they seek (Matthew 6:33). Earlier in the Sermon on the Mount, He employed the same word to urge His listeners to make reconciling conflicts a priority before trying to engage in worship or giving (5:24). He also used the same term to show that those who would correct the blindness of others must "first remove the plank from your own eye" (7:5).

Jesus employed this term to warn us not to allow distractions to keep us from making our relationship with Him our top priority (Luke 9:59–61). Two individuals professed a desire to follow Him, then said, "Let me first take care of some other pressing need." One wanted to bury his father first—probably the father was still living and he wished to care for his aging parent. The other wished to say his good-byes to those at home before leaving to follow Jesus. The Master's strong response to each demonstrated His concern that no follower of His allow other things to become the priority.

The Lord also used the term in Matthew 22:38 and three times in Mark 12:28–30 to underscore the "priority commandments" of loving God and our neighbor. Paul used this same word in 2 Corinthians 8:5 to show how the Philippians made giving themselves to the Lord the priority even before giving of their resources. He also used it to warn Timothy that widows who would serve in the church were to first show piety at home and care for their parents (1 Timothy 5:4).

Finally, Jesus used the word five times as He introduced the Revelation to John on the island of Patmos. He referred to Himself as "the first and the last" and warned believers who had left their first love to "repent and do the first works" (Revelation 2:4–5). It seems that Jesus wanted to show how easy it is to neglect the priority of loving Him wholeheartedly. Since He is the "first and the last," we need to make cultivating our relationship with Him our top priority.

The priority of the believer's relationship with Christ seems to have been Paul's objective in his use of the word *skopeō,* which means "a mark or point of focus." Paul used the noun form to describe his personal life goal of being approved by Christ (Philippians 3:14) and the verb to indicate that our objective must be to serve others rather than our own interests (Philippians 2:4) and to show how the eternal rather than the temporal must be our ultimate focus (2 Corinthians 4:18).

FIVE CRUCIAL AREAS

Our usual approach is to express the priorities as Christ first, then family, followed by church, then job or career, then other areas of life. Christian management consultant Doug Sherman and coauthor Bill Hendricks have proposed an alternative to this frequently taught "hierarchy of Christian priorities." They suggest that, if we make a list of personal

 **STRESS TEST** . . . .

A Balancing Act

How satisfied are you with where you stand in each of the five areas we've been looking at? Think about the time you've invested in each, how successful you have been in bringing them under biblical guidelines, and how effective you have been in each one. Rate each from 1 to 10, with 10 being the most successful.

Personal Life

1   2   3   4   5   6   7   8   9   10

Family

1   2   3   4   5   6   7   8   9   10

Church

1   2   3   4   5   6   7   8   9   10

Employment

1   2   3   4   5   6   7   8   9   10

Community and Social Life

1   2   3   4   5   6   7   8   9   10

Look at each item and determine which ones need improvement. You might want to ask your spouse or a good friend how he or she would rank you.

. . . .

priorities, Christ shouldn't be on it. Instead, He should be the Lord over everything on the list.

The Sherman-Hendricks alternative involves what they describe as "the pentathlon, a comprehensive view of five crucial areas of life using the illustration of the athlete who trains in all five areas of the European pentathlon—running, swimming, horseback riding, pistol shooting, and fencing."⁸ They recommend that believers focus on five key applicational areas found in the practical sections of most of Paul's letters—personal life, family, church, employment, and community and social life. They observe, "Because they all impact each, we cannot arrange them into a hierarchy. The New Testament does not do that and if we do it it will actually hinder us from being faithful in all five areas. Instead, we need to strike a realistic balance among these areas, each of which presents many demands that compete for our time."⁹

Here's a practical suggestion to help you follow this balanced strategy for prioritizing your life. Use your concordance to find passages of Scripture relating to work, particularly in Paul's epistles. Your search can include "work," "slaves," "masters," or other related concepts. Select a few and study them extensively to learn how they apply to these key areas of life, including your work. Determine how each will impact the two major priorities of life—loving God wholeheartedly and loving people unconditionally.

BALANCE FROM THE PSALMIST

In Psalm 27 David recognized that a host of enemies threatened his life. However, his confident trust in the Lord gave him insight and strength to wait for God's provision and overcome his fears (vv. 1–3). Then in verse 4, David expressed a positive statement of his life mission, with God as the focal point: "One thing have I desired of the Lord, that will I seek: that I may dwell in the house of the Lord all the days of my life, to behold the beauty of the Lord, and to inquire in His temple." The word he used for "one thing" is the Hebrew numeral one, found hundreds of times in the Old Testament. By his use of the simple term, David was saying that God had become the number-one priority of his life.

The term David used for "seek," *baqash,* was used frequently in the Old Testament with such meanings as seek to find, seek to secure, aim at or practice, seek the face (as of rulers or of God), desire, or require.[10] Solomon used it to explain the importance of seeking wisdom the way others seek for silver and gold (Proverbs 2:2–4), to show the value of seeking knowledge (15:14), and as part of the maxim "those who seek the Lord understand all" (28:5). It clearly indicates priority, especially when taken with the numeral one.

Notice what David established as his priorities. The first was "to dwell in the Lord's house all the days of my life." For the psalmist, remaining in God's house was equivalent to staying in fellowship with the Lord, since for David the tabernacle and temple signified God's physical presence on earth. What he was expressing was the counterpart of our saying "I want to maintain close, personal contact with the Lord."

Second, David wanted to behold the beauty of the Lord. David's point extended beyond physical beauty and expressed the psalmist's desire to remain focused on the beauty of God's person. In a sense, David sounded like a lonely soldier or business traveler who keeps a picture of his beloved posted in a prominent place to remind him of the beauty of the person he loves and the priority of the relationship.

The third facet of David's statement stressed his goal "to inquire in His temple." The *New American Standard* translates this phrase "and to meditate in His temple." The word used at the end of the verse comes from a root that means to plow and has the idea of inspecting, admiring, or seeking out. Another root conveys the idea of striving after; desiring, getting, or requiring.[11] The concept of inquiring as meditating or seeking God's direction certainly carries practical implications for believers today. If we are to base our life on a biblical foundation, we must understand what the Scripture says about the various areas that touch our lives.

Bruce Neuharth, whose story we considered earlier, illustrates this principle in his life: "I recently concluded the two most difficult weeks of my four years at Godfather's or at any other time during my management career. I had to dismiss several members of my staff due to a substantial budget cutback. God taught me a lot of important lessons as I wrestled with the responsibility of laying off several key people, including two managers. In the past, the stress would have been almost unbearable; but in this situation, I realized I could call on God for help. One of the first questions I asked myself was, 'How would Christ handle this situation?' That didn't remove the unpleasantness but it enabled me to deal with the people affected in a more caring, sensitive manner."[12]

Bruce explained that the Bible had become his most important resource for life. "Whenever I find myself struggling in my job, I am always reminded to check my focus, determining whether I am trying to deal with my circumstances from God's perspective or going back to my old ways of trying to handle them myself." Like David of old, Bruce Neuharth had discovered the secret of divine peace and direction for work and life. "Commit your way to the Lord, trust also in Him, and He shall bring it to pass" (Psalm 37:5).

SPECIFIC STEPS

For those of us who face the challenges of workplace stress today, the key question involves how to implement David's strategy into our lives and careers. How does God expect us to plug His priority into the variety of pressures, essentials, and urgencies we face? Perhaps the place to begin is with the question we were all asked as children: What do you want to do with your life? What would you like to be when you grow up? *But I'm already grown up!* you protest. In fact, you explain, you feel trapped in a job that doesn't give much of an opportunity to make God a priority.

I recall when someone asked me if I had a life mission. My quick reply was, "Sure I do. It's to glorify God and do everything in a way that pleases Him." Now that's a great generality, but I realized it wasn't very specific. So I decided to step back and spend some time evaluating my life. I asked myself, What are my primary gifts? How has God designed me so that I can best serve and glorify Him? How can I use my energies and abilities with maximum vocational impact?

Out of that reflection came a life mission statement that focused on the gift of encouragement. I have come to consider my life mission to be "to demonstrate wholehearted love for God and unconditional love for people by providing biblical encouragement through preaching and teaching, radio and writing, as well as personal contact with people."

That sounds simple and straightforward, but it took some time for me to work it out. First, I needed to confirm that my primary gift was in the area of encouragement. I had suspected this, and others who knew me well confirmed it. I needed to integrate my giftedness into those two most important mandates of life, loving God wholeheartedly and loving people unconditionally. I also needed to look at ways God had provided for me to express and use my giftedness, such as preaching, broadcasting, and writing.

Out of this I wrote my life mission statement. According to Stephen Covey, developing a mission statement empowers us to live against the grain of both our environment and our own ingrained habits or scripts. In other words, we can "act instead of being acted upon as the passion of vision gives us a new understanding of independent will."[13] The priority of a life mission driving us from within makes it easier for us to say no to what is less important and focus on priorities, streamlining our lives and reducing stress.

Point of Perspective

So how does this connect with my work? I recognize the ultimate priority of my relationship with Jesus Christ, understanding who He is and how He wants me to most effectively serve Him. I look at every detail of my life—my work, my relationships with family, my contact with friends, my relationships at church—as an extension of my ultimate mission in life. Thus, wherever I am, whatever I'm doing, that overall objective must give my life meaning and perspective and guide all my responses and decisions.

My friend Tim calls on farmers in Hill County in central Texas. He lives in the county seat, Hillsboro, and drives thirty or more miles in all directions. Tim told me about an interesting lesson his job taught him about Hill County geography. No matter where you drive in the county, it's possible to tell where you are by noting your location in reference to the courthouse. The tallest building for miles around, it towers over downtown Hillsboro and the surrounding landscape. If you can't see it from wherever you happen to be, you can generally spot it by driving a short distance. The courthouse provides a great resource, keeping Tim oriented whether he's driving in the northeast, northwest, southwest, or southeast part of the county.

In the same way, whether at work, relating to someone in the neighborhood, or spending time with family, the priority of my relationship with Christ can keep me focused. My mission statement both empowers and directs me: anything I do that doesn't fit it is counterproductive, whether at work, in my family relationships, my church life, my personal life, or my social life. Instead of getting caught in the trap of so many high-powered management books and seminars that teach me ways to pack more work into my schedule or how to trim more activities from my life, I come to grips with the larger question of how work fits in with the rest of life.

Big Rocks

A second practical step involves learning to tell the difference between the big rocks and the little ones. Remember the Stephen Covey story about putting the big rocks in the jar first? It's so easy to get wrapped up in putting little rocks in little jars, or even little rocks in big jars. All the little and large things—even urgent things—fit better when we learn to make the "big rock" priorities most important. That's why both Paul and David focused on their relationship with the Lord and made that which is eternal most important.

This underscores the importance of looking to the Word for answers. The problem is, most of us have learned to settle for a restricted diet of the Word that leaves us spiritually malnourished at best. Yet the more we feed ourselves on a balanced diet of the Word, the better equipped we become to deal with specific problems in a way consistent with our ultimate mission and priorities.

Some time ago I came across an article written by William Biggs, an electrical engineer and president of Li-Cor Incorporated. After three years as an electronics engineer with the University of Nebraska and two with a local Bell Labs affiliate, he started his own company, manufacturing high-tech plant research instruments.

By his own admission Bill was a chronic worrier. "While starting out, I worried about whether I would ever achieve success. Once I was successful, I worried about future failure. When there was nothing to be concerned about, I worried about that."[14] In 1978 Bill came to faith in Christ. But this didn't bring an immediate end to his worries and fears. Even after he learned to consult Christ in his day-to-day decisions, he still struggled with the "who's in control" question.

For Bill, the solution came from learning the psalmist's approach to handling the stresses of life—reviewing and trusting the promises of God. As he explained, "Everyone seems to be looking for a cure or antidote to stress. They try medication, relaxation exercise, alcohol, drugs, and countless other devices or diversions. I found the best solution was to focus on God and His promises. I compiled a packet of twenty-five cards designed to help me and others achieve a closer relationship to the Lord, enabling us to draw on the sustaining life of Jesus Christ."[15] For Bill, using these cards to remember what God's Word says about seeking God, abiding in Christ, handling trials, trusting God's promises, and praying effectively has caused him to replace time spent worrying with time meditating on the Word. As he concedes, "We will never escape stress entirely, but what a difference it makes when we learn to concentrate on Christ and the promises of Scripture instead of on the crisis at hand."

Another key resource is memorizing Scripture. I couldn't begin to count the number of times a verse or passage I committed to memory years earlier provided me with the help I needed to deal with some source of stress at work.

Crucial Balance

A third principle I need for my stress-relieving strategy is to learn to establish balance between the crucial areas of life. For those of us who tend to be driven by priorities and focused on achievement, this may be difficult. One of the most important lessons I have learned in recent years is to develop balance in my schedule. I haven't totally arrived in this area, but I've come a long way. At one time I found it difficult, if not impossible, to leave the office with any project undone. I also felt guilty whenever I took time off. Now I have practical strategies to help me balance these work demands and still fulfill my life mission.

One practical step is to look at what you pour your energy into during your time away from work. Recently I visited in the home of Brad, the CEO of a large company. Brad is committed to making his family a priority. He is also a hard worker. I noticed that Brad spent a lot of his time at home concentrating on things from work. He brought home a packed briefcase, talked at length with associates on the phone about work-related issues, and spent most of his time with his wife discussing work-related pressures.

After visiting in his home, I felt prompted to go back and evaluate how I was spending my time with my family off the job. With the encouragement and help of my wife and some close friends, I determined to minimize work-related concentration at home. I decided to try to practice what my friend Brian Erickson, our chief operating officer at Back to the Bible, told me he intended to use as his policy for vacation. "I'm going to listen to our broadcast," Brian had said, "primarily because it ministers to me. But I intend to spend my vacation weeks totally separated from the pressures of work. They'll still be there when I get back, but I don't need to take them home with me. Carol and I are going to enjoy our family and our time of leisure."

Another key to regaining control of our schedules involves planning and scheduling for nonwork activities the same way we do for work. Many of us practice discipline and establish priorities in our work, yet take a much more casual approach to personal and family time. We need to write down appointments with our spouses and children, schedule specific activities for evenings rather than taking the "Let's see what's on television tonight" routine, and make sure we cultivate areas of active interest such as hiking or bicycling instead of becoming couch potatoes.

A fourth suggestion, perhaps the one with the greatest practical impact, involves learning to gain our personal significance from our relationship with Christ rather than from our performance on the job. I hosted a radio program in which Terry Bolt of the Rapha Christian Counseling organization discussed how false beliefs undermine our emotional and spiritual well-being. As we talked with people from all over the country, we discovered a common theme, one eloquently expressed by a caller from Ohio: "I find myself driven at work, church, even in relationships. No matter what I do it's not quite enough. How do I get off this treadmill?"

Bolt asked the caller, "Where do you find your personal significance—from your relationship with Christ or from your performance?" It took just a few diagnostic questions before our listener admitted that performance had become his most important priority. He felt driven to be the best Christian, father, worker, and citizen he could possibly be. And since he had only twenty-four hours in the day instead of thirty or thirty-two, he wasn't succeeding very well.

Bolt recommended that our caller recognize that who he is as a person isn't based on either performance or the approval of others. Instead, personal value and worth come from understanding what it means to be loved, accepted, and forgiven by Christ. When we realize that our personal significance is wrapped up in Him, when we focus on the mission He has given us, when we learn to make specific choices that relate to Him and to His Word, and when we understand how to set limits and achieve balance among the variety of roles and relationships God has given us in life, then we have reached a position where our work and other areas of our life will become much less stressful.

I remember hearing Chuck Swindoll on his radio program "Insight for Living" observe how we "worship our work, work at our play, and play at our worship." May God give us the vision to keep personal worship, work, and play balanced in a way that will glorify God and fulfill His mission for our lives.

Linda Becker, our human resources manager, expressed it this way: "For most people, work provides significance here on earth. But I think work is where we can manifest to others who God is to us all day long. It's an opportunity to show God's character to the people we work with and a way to be used as a tool. Whether we work in a Christian workplace or a secular environment, the bottom line is, whatever we do in word or deed, we are to do all to the glory of God."

Turning Over Control

Our final principle involves turning control of everything over to the Lord. The key to surrendering control of circumstances to God is trust—trusting God's ability to determine what is best, relying on the rightness of His direction, allowing Him to order the big and little things in our lives by following His Word carefully and obeying Him without question. David learned those lessons when he stopped fretting or whimpering over the pressures and circumstances he faced.

Like the psalmist, I must recognize my inability to figure

out what's going on, give up my jealousy toward those who seem to be faring better than I, and quit responding with evil actions to get even (Psalm 37:1–2). Like David I have to learn the basic lesson of trusting in the Lord, relying on Him the way David explained in Psalm 37. Such trust expresses itself in several important ways.

First, I learn to do good. It is not enough just to verbalize my trust in the Lord. Trusting Him leads to obedience. The song "Trust and Obey" links these two important concepts, recognizing them as a key to happiness in Jesus.

Second, I am to delight in the Lord. Some people delight in their children or grandchildren—Kathy and I certainly do —whereas others take delight in a new car, a delicious meal, or their fiancé(e). For David, delight came from his relationship with the Lord, seeing Him not as a cruel taskmaster but as a delightful Friend with whom he enjoyed spending time.

David also learned to commit his way to the Lord. The word translated "commit" parallels the concept of trust, and literally means to roll your burden or way over onto the Lord. Instead of trying to control the future, we are to place it confidently in His hands.

The final two concepts David expressed in Psalm 37—rest in the Lord and wait patiently for Him—are closely connected. David had learned to wait on the Lord rather than becoming agitated, griping, or complaining. His outward responses reflected his inward attitude of patience and showed confidence in God's ultimate control of circumstances or life.

Waiting is something not many of us are good at doing. I know I've spent many a restless hour awaiting delayed flights at airports, and God has used those stressful delays to teach me valuable lessons. After all, there are worse alternatives to a flight delayed by bad weather or mechanical problems!

PRACTICAL OUTWORKING

So what does making God the priority in our lives look like in practical terms? Perhaps the best place to find the biblical answer to this question is in the application section of the book of Colossians. In that epistle, as in no other, Paul presents Christ as the ultimate priority, pointing out that "in all things He may [should] have the preeminence" (1:18). His person and work are represented as the antidote for theological error in the first two chapters of the letter. Then in chapter 3 Paul begins to explain the practical implications of the Master's preeminence. After calling for a new perspective ("Seek those things which are above," vv. 1–4) and a new lifestyle ("Put off the old, put on the new," vv. 5–15), the apostle explains three practical priorities that can demonstrate where we have put Christ in our lives.

First, when Christ is preeminent, His peace rules in our hearts (Colossians 3:15). Paul has already explained our positional peace in Christ (1:19–22). Now he talks about two other facets of this truth: personal peace of mind, the absence of worry; and practical peace, getting along with each other. Just as an official keeps rowdy fans and heated combatants under control at a baseball game or tennis match, so the peace of Christ produces both internal and interpersonal harmony in our lives.

Second, when Christ occupies first place, the Word of Christ is at home in our lives (Colossians 3:16). Paul isn't simply advocating an academic knowledge of the Word. He wants the Word to be at home in our personal experience. The phrase "at home" carries the idea of being both familiar with and comfortable with. When we lived in Louisiana and Texas, we were "at home" with foods like jambalaya, crawfish étouffée, sausage gumbo, and dark roast coffee, eggs, and grits for breakfast. On the other hand, since we have enjoyed quite a bit of lamb, we are comfortable eating roast leg of lamb in a way many Britons are, but few Nebraskans.

Paul is calling for our lives to conform to the Word so that it will be comfortably "at home" in our experience. How does this come about? He lists two specific ways—positive teaching and practical admonishment—and suggests that music is often involved, since songs, hymns, and spiritual songs produce gratitude in our hearts.

Third, when Christ occupies the priority position, His name will be demonstrated by our conduct (Colossians 3:17). Paul points out that whatever we do—including worship in the local church, our employment, and our family relationships—should demonstrate the character of the Lord Jesus, our association with Him, and our submission to His authority. In other words, doing things "in His name" includes both submission to His authority and reflection of His character. This in turn produces a lifestyle that demonstrates gratitude for all He has done for us.

I once heard someone put it very well. In the world there are three kinds of people. There are many to whom Jesus Christ means nothing. They have never trusted Him as their Savior. Then there are those to whom Christ means something. They have trusted Him, perhaps they've even started walking with Him at some level. Finally, there are those who have mastered priority living. To them, Jesus Christ means everything. His peace rules in their hearts. His Word is at home in their lives, and His name is reflected in everything they do. Their priority focus helps them make the choices that can put a significant dent in stress in the workplace.

CHAPTER ELEVEN

ATTITUDES AND MOTIVATION

The other day several of us were talking at lunch about a lady who is old enough to be our mother, even though each of us has lived to fifty or beyond. We all agreed that the lady is one of the sweetest, most gracious individuals we know. Whenever I have spoken in our church she has always had a word of cheer and encouragement for me. She has also encouraged my wife on many occasions.

One of my colleagues at Back to the Bible told how, when the lady in question found out about a major change in our ministry, her comment was a cheerful, "Well, that's not what I'd like to see done, but I'm sure they've prayed about it and feel they are doing what the Lord wants them to do." I hope I have that kind of winning attitude when I reach her age.

Attitudes and motivation play such a crucial role in our work and our lives. There are many things you can change just by the way you look at them.

Remember the lesson we learned in chapter 6? Stress is composed of three major components—the event itself, or the stressor; your physiological response, often called fight-or-flight; and and most important component, your mental perception, or how you view the stressor.

The Apollo 13 space mission barely escaped disaster. Throughout a seven-day ordeal following an onboard explosion, astronauts Jim Lovell, Fred Haise, and Jack Swigert spent many hours in cold and dark, not knowing if they would ever have a chance to reactivate their spacecraft and survive reentry. The major news networks interviewed a series of "experts," most of whom talked about how little chance the men had of surviving while explaining in great detail the various ways the mission could fail.

The men in the spacecraft and Houston's mission control, under the leadership of Harvey Kranz, never gave up in the face of adversity. They maintained their composure and their resolve. What could have been NASA's greatest disaster up to that time turned out to be what Kranz referred to as her finest hour.

ATTITUDE'S IMPACT

But is this business of approaching things with a positive mind-set overrated? Can we really make a difference in what we do on the job or how we handle problem people just by getting motivated and developing a positive attitude?

The answer to that question isn't the simple yes or no we might prefer. Well-known motivational speaker Zig Ziglar talks about this issue to tens of thousands of people every year. As he delivers his message of humor, hope, and enthusiasm to people all over the world, he points out that "positive thinking enables you to maximize your skill, but all the positive thinking in the world will not carry a golf ball through the trees, over the pond and around the sand trap, if the skill necessary to execute the shot is not present."[1]

So what will positive thinking let you do? It allows you to use your ability and experience to the maximum. According to Ziglar that's a realistic expectation, but "to believe that positive thinking will let you do anything is tantamount to disaster. It is untrue and very damaging because it creates false hope and unrealistic expectations."[2] Ziglar observes that many bankruptcies are filed every year by people who conceived what they believed to be marvelous ideas and believed with all their heart they could achieve them. But Ziglar says that, when you combine a positive attitude with persistence, enthusiasm, and hope, the end result is both an improvement in attitude and an increase in performance.

Several years ago while visiting Zig at his office, I was introduced to a young man named John Foppe. Later I wrote a magazine article about John, which I titled "His Own Pair of Hands." The title had a dual meaning: it told how a national organization presented John with the Helping Hands Award for his efforts to help others and how this young man in his twenties had been born without arms.

John and his parents were faced with a choice over how they could handle his lack of arms. He didn't even have the option to throw up his hands and quit, although he and his parents could have given up on life. Instead, they chose to look beyond what could be considered a total disaster and began searching for solutions.

John showed me some of the pictures he has drawn—he is a far more talented artist than many people who have both hands. He has learned to handle many seemingly impossible tasks, such as driving a car, cooking, and shaving, because of his determination and adaptability. He worked hard to finish college in less than four years, graduated with honors, and developed a career speaking to church, school, and business audiences all over the country. He was invited to become a member of the Ziglar Corporation's speaker team after he shared the platform with Zig at the National Quality and Business Development Foundation meeting in 1990.

I recall the day I sat in John's office, looked at his paintings, and listened to the story of the change in attitude that changed his life. As a ten-year-old, John had received a great deal of assistance from his family. He came to believe that his disadvantage meant that he was entitled to have all his needs met by others.

Then one day his mother put a stop to all the help John had been receiving. When she did, John promptly threw what he later referred to as a heavy-duty pity party. At that point his mother placed a newspaper story before him about a little girl who had neither arms nor feet. As John put it, "That day I started looking at what I had instead of what I didn't have." For John it was the beginning of a positive attitude that led to hard work and produced incredible achievement.

ATTITUDE CHECKUP

Perhaps you are still thinking, "I just don't buy this attitude business, Don. Positive thinking may work for motivational speakers, but it's just not biblical." When I checked my concordance, I discovered fifteen Old Testament words translated "to think," plus eleven more Greek terms from the New Testament[3]—and that doesn't even include the words that mean to think evil of or think good of.

Solomon provided a biblical foundation when he pointed out that our thinking demonstrates our true nature. You have probably heard the maxim repeated many times that you are what you eat. The parallel truth in the immaterial realm is just as true—we are what we think. Consider the implications for dealing with workplace stress. What you put into your mind, the thoughts you dwell on, affect who you are and what you do, including your responses to stress.

Furthermore, Scripture commands us to regulate our thought life. As Paul said in 1 Corinthians 13:11, "When I was a child, I spoke as a child, I understood as a child, I thought as a child; but when I became a man, I put away childish things." Our thoughts should reflect our maturity in Christ.

This happens as our thoughts become aligned with Scripture. In John 5:39 Jesus told His disciples to search the Scriptures "for in them you think you have eternal life; and these are they which testify of Me." The word translated "think" can also mean "to seem or appear." Paul used it in Galatians 6:3 to show that a man who thinks himself to be something that

 **STRESS TEST**

Your Attitude Is Showing

Consider each statement, and determine how much it describes you or how often it is true of you, especially when you are in a stressful work situation. Rate each from 1 to 10.

I do not compromise the truth or engage in deception.

1   2   3   4   5   6   7   8   9   10

I do the right thing even when it may be harmful to my job security or career.

1   2   3   4   5   6   7   8   9   10

I try to be a friend to my co-workers or peers.

1   2   3   4   5   6   7   8   9   10

I interact with my co-workers in a fair and consistent manner.

1   2   3   4   5   6   7   8   9   10

I do not engage in workplace gossip.

1   2   3   4   5   6   7   8   9   10

I find things to praise about my co-workers or those I manage.

1   2   3   4   5   6   7   8   9   10

I am a positive influence on my co-workers or those I manage.

1   2   3   4   5   6   7   8   9   10

I pray for my co-workers, peers, or those I manage.

1   2   3   4   5   6   7   8   9   10

I exhibit a thankful, rather than complaining, spirit at work.

1   2   3   4   5   6   7   8   9   10

The truly successful person is the one whose attitudes translate into godly actions and relationships. Such a person experiences less stress in the workplace.

he isn't deceives himself. And James employed the word to urge us not to take Scripture's warnings lightly (James 4:5).

THOUGHT-LIFE CHECKLIST

The common New Testament word *logizomai* means to think about or process something logically. It is used in 1 Corinthians 13:11 of childish mental processes. Paul used it four times in 2 Corinthians to challenge his readers to think carefully about themselves and his apostolic ministry.

In what may be the ultimate biblical commentary on the subject, Paul used *logizomai* in Philippians 4 to instruct us regarding the Christian's proper thought life. He gives a mental inventory or checklist—a grid through which to evaluate the myriad thoughts that pass through our minds every day.

The apostle had called on his friends at Philippi to stand fast, demonstrate unity, rejoice in the Lord, and replace anxious worries with steadfast prayer (Philippians 4:1–6). If they followed these instructions, he promises, the peace of God will be established in their hearts and minds (v. 7).

The problem is, for them—and for us today—peace of mind is an elusive quality incompatible with the turmoil of chronic anxiety. That's why Paul's exhortation to replace worry with continual prayer has such practical benefit for those of us who constantly worry about some aspect of our work or lives without ever really commiting it to the Lord in prayer.

Then Paul draws an important analogy. He pictures our minds as resembling a battleground, with thoughts like bullets flying in all directions. Some originate in God, others in Satan. As the apostle wrote in 2 Corinthians 10:5, we are to take every thought captive to the obedience of Christ.

And how are we to do this? By using Paul's checklist or mental survey for evaluating our thoughts: "Finally, brethren, whatever things are true, whatever things are noble, whatever things are just, whatever things are pure, whatever things are lovely, whatever things are of good report, if there is any virtue and if there is anything praiseworthy—meditate on these things" (Philippians 4:8).

Notice that the checklist doesn't begin with the question "Is it positive or negative?" but "Is it true?" Since God is characterized by truth and Satan is the ultimate liar, it is important for our thoughts to focus on that which is true.

Have you noticed that we live in an era of illusion? Several years ago, when I was managing a Christian radio station in Kansas City, the city's Public Health Director, Dr. Richard Biery, told me "the rest of the story" about what had been described by local television reports the night before as a riot in his office. "There were only five protesters," he explained. "But they knew how to play the camera angles just right."

Creation scientist Ken Ham deals with this issue almost daily in his ministry. As he explained to me, "There are so many Christians who are convinced that evolution is true, that the Bible account of creation must be accommodated or 'stretched' to fit billions of years, dinosaurs, and fossils. Don, it just isn't true. There is no scientific evidence, including Carbon 14 dating, that demands billions of years or contradicts the Genesis record of creation in six literal days and a worldwide flood." In this issue as in others, truth is crucial.

Next Paul asks, Does the issue have substance? The word translated "noble" in Philippians 4:8 carries the idea of that which is substantial. It's so easy for us to fill our minds with "mental junk food." Much of what we hear on radio and television or read today carries the mental nutritional value of cotton candy or greasy potato chips. Recently my son Brent and I worked our way through *Mere Christianity* by C. S. Lewis. "This is really solid stuff, Dad," he told me.

Third, is what we are thinking about right or just? So often in our day we look for the expedient or easy way out of tough or complex situations rather than having the courage to do the right thing. Doing what's right begins with thinking what's right. When we hear that choice bit of office gossip, will we nod agreement, ignore the situation, or investigate the facts and lovingly confront those who are speaking out of turn?

Fourth, is what we are thinking about pure? Remember the old computer adage "Garbage in, garbage out"? Unfortunately most of us have collected—and continue to collect—so much mental refuse that we have trouble getting it out of our minds! This includes the garbage of gossip, backstabbing, and what Paul called "corrupt communication."

Fifth, are our thoughts loving? The term *lovely* describes that which demonstrates or communicates love. We need to close our minds to ugly thoughts of vindictiveness, bitterness, and hostility and open them to the beauty of thoughts that demonstrate authentic love for God and people. Our minds are bombarded with a constant stream of data, including the caustic comments we often hear at work about the stupidity of management or the plans to produce a work slowdown on the assembly line. Such messages need to be carefully filtered through our biblical "thought-screener."

Sixth, are our thoughts of good report? For years the *New York Times* carried the slogan "All the news that's fit to print." Sadly, a few years ago the *Times* carried, on adjacent pages, the story of a lower court ruling against the distribution of Scripture portions in a school classroom and the account of plans to distribute condoms in another school system! We need to be sure the reports we allow to pass through our mind and verbalize with our lips are consistent with what God calls good.

Seventh, does what we are thinking reflect excellence or moral virtue? In other words, how clean is it? In these days of *E. coli* scares in fast-food restaurants and supermarkets, most of us are careful to cook our beef until all harmful bacteria have been killed. We also need to guard our minds against the moral pollution of the cesspool-like world around us.

Finally, do our thoughts carry praise? It's so easy to be critical and sarcastic, thinking negatively about others. Here's where we can provide positive perspective on the issues we think about. That doesn't mean we refuse to look at reality or to face the fact that some things are negative. On the other hand, it does mean, when we have the option to view the glass as half full or half empty, we choose to see it half full.

Crucial Terms

Some time ago I heard Chuck Swindoll make a profound statement about attitudes on his radio program "Insight for Living." He pointed out that attitude is more important than facts, than the past, than education, than money, than circumstances, than failures, than successes, than what other people think or say or do. It is more important than appearance, ability, or skill. According to Chuck Swindoll, attitude can make or break a company, a church, or a home.

Swindoll went on to explain that every day we have a choice regarding the attitudes we embrace. We cannot change our past or the fact that people will respond in a certain way, but we can change our own attitudes. Life is 10 percent what happens to me and 90 percent how I react to it! In other words, we are in charge of our attitudes.

One biblical example of a man with right attitudes was John the Baptist. He made his attitude toward sin clear when he called on the religious leaders and others of his generation to repent and by their actions to prove that repentance. He demonstrated the right attitude toward himself when he said, "[Christ] must increase, but I must decrease" (John 3:30). In saying this, he also expressed the right attitude toward the Savior. Pointing people to Christ was John's focus throughout his ministry. We see it in his words "Behold! The Lamb of God who takes away the sin of the world!" (1:29).

The apostle Paul provides us with another example of how proper attitudes can affect our lives. In Philippians 4, he explained his God-given ability to live independent of circumstances (v. 11). The Spirit of God had let him in on an important secret that allowed him to live contentedly in any situation, whether humiliated or abounding, in need or possessing everything (v. 12). The secret is an attitude that confidently affirms, "I can do all things through Christ who strengthens me" (v. 13). This attitude demonstrates the crucial balance needed for true positive thinking. The apostle didn't say, "Christ can do all things and I'm zero." Nor did he claim, "I can do everything. Christ must be so proud of me!"

Instead, his statement reflected the perfect balance of a man who recognized that God had gifted him to handle every situation, but who ultimately recognized his total dependence on Christ who empowered him. This is exactly the kind of confident, positive faith God wants us to apply to our work and our lives today.

MOTIVATION

This brings us to the subject of motivation, since attitude ultimately leads to motivation. During Paul's first visit to the city of Philippi, he demonstrated the kind of attitude he later wrote about in his epistle. He and his partner Silas had been locked up in the local jail—and it wasn't one of those minimum-security "country club" facilities frequented by the white-collar criminals of our day. Paul and Silas were totally undeserving of such treatment. They had simply been trying to serve God and the people of Philippi. The experience wasn't pleasant, and, for all they knew, their lives were on the line! So what did they do? Sit and sulk? Gripe and complain?

Scripture tells us that their positive attitude motivated them to pray and sing praises to the Lord. In fact, they probably kept their fellow prisoners awake! Ultimately their jailer came to faith and they were released to continue the Lord's work. Attitude plus motivation had made the difference.

We see this same principle illustrated in the Old Testament experience of Daniel's three companions, Hananiah, Mishael, and Azariah. (I prefer their Jewish names to the idol-based Shadrach, Meshach, and Abed-nego.) Their positive attitude and commitment to worship only the Lord kept them from bowing to the golden image Nebuchadnezzar had made.

When the king offered them a second chance to worship the statue, they again refused and pointed out their confidence in God's ability to deliver them (Daniel 3:17). However, as they unequivocably told the king, even if the Lord chose not to protect them from the fiery furnace, they refused to worship any idol.

Their testimony, like Daniel's when he was thrown into the lion's den, demonstrated a positive trust in God's ability, plus the conviction that it's essential to always do what is right. That's why Daniel's remarkable career in public service lasted so long. He maintained a diligent approach to his work, kept his attitude positive, remained supportive of his bosses, yet always conducted himself in a way that reflected his convictions, integrity, and trust in the God of Israel.

Like Daniel, Nehemiah was a Jewish man who held an important position serving a foreign king. His attitude toward sin and its consequences was expressed by his grief and unhappiness as he prayed and fasted before God over the condition of the city of his people. When King Artaxerxes asked about his sad countenance, Nehemiah immediately lifted a prayer to God, took courage, and voiced his urgent concern about his city, even at the risk of the king's displeasure. The result: "The king granted [the things I had requested] according to the good hand of my God upon me" (Nehemiah 2:8).

Throughout the book that bears his name, Nehemiah demonstrated a balanced attitude. He exercised diligence, hard work, leadership, and organizational skills, yet he constantly recognized that "the hand of my God [was] good upon me" (see Nehemiah 2:18). He was able to motivate the residents of Jerusalem to join him in the effort to rebuild the city walls. When opposition developed, he addressed their issues, claimed God's grace and power, and committed himself and his people to the task at hand without allowing the opposition to become a distraction to the work. He refused to allow his opponents to stop the work by ridicule (4:1–3), nor did he permit those on the workforce to engage in negative thinking and thereby discourage their colleagues (4:10–14). Instead, he devised a plan to compensate for their weaknesses, and he reminded them of the strength and power of their God (v. 14). Due to Nehemiah's persistent motivation, the massive task of rebuilding the walls of Jerusalem was completed in just fifty-two days (6:15).

Throughout his political career, Abraham Lincoln demonstrated a remarkable attitude and motivation. He refused to allow bitterness to cloud his thinking. When he was elected to the presidency, he began listing men to appoint to his cabinet. When he proposed the name of one of his fiercest detractors, a man who had frequently assailed his character during the campaign, his colleagues listed all the things this man had done to harm Lincoln's reputation. "Don't you remember . . ." they said over and over.

Lincoln is said to have replied, "I distinctly remember forgetting those things."

This story serves as a classic reminder that attitude is a choice. So, too, is motivation. Motivation is that which drives us or, as some like to put it, "turns our crank."

So how does motivation work? Christian management authority Ted Engstrom explains that "to motivate others is to infuse in people a spirit of eagerness to perform effectively. As you discipline yourself to become a motivated person, others will be inspired through your example and the work you do."[4] Engstrom cites several motivational tools, including encouragement, participation, recognition, and praise.

When Engstrom faces personal hindrances, he has a two-step plan for self-motivation. The first step is "to remind myself that God has created me in His own image, recognizing God's empowerment. The second step is to come up with small increments of action that will allow me to begin doing whatever it is that can't be done."[5] Not only has Ted Engstrom motivated himself through this action plan, but his organization, World Vision, has used the plan to feed seventy-six thousand refugees in Somalia, East Africa, "one at a time."

Motivation was a key factor for the apostle Paul as well. First, he chose not to be moved by the adverse circumstances of life. When he addressed the elders of the church at Ephesus, he spoke of the uncertainty of what he faced en route to Jerusalem and of the danger of imprisonment that awaited him. Then he added, "but none of these things move me; nor do I count my life dear to myself, so that I may finish my race with joy, and the ministry which I received of the Lord Jesus, to testify to the gospel of the grace of God" (Acts 20:24).

Paul refused to allow other factors to hinder his motivational drive to finish the itinerary God had planned for his life. The word he used for "finish my course" implied the planned itinerary of a ship. Paul had fulfilled God's mandate to preach the gospel (Acts 20:25), to teach the whole counsel of God to believers (v. 27), and to preach Christ where His name had not been preached before (Romans 15:19–20).

Aparently Paul demonstrated positive attitude and motivation in his career as a tentmaker, for we never hear of any complaints about his work or of conflict between him and his colleagues Priscilla and Aquilla.

IMPACT TODAY

So what about attitude and motivation today? How can they affect our lives? Some practical suggestions are in order.

First, we need to maintain a positive "I can do all things through Christ" attitude even during times of failure. Just a week after Jim Sundburg helped the Kansas City Royals win the 1985 World Series, I interviewed him in a radio studio in Dallas, Texas. We talked about baseball averages and how this All Star had experienced ups and downs during his thirteen-year major league career. After being named Most Valuable Player for the Texas Rangers in 1977, his batting average dropped and he was traded unexpectedly—first to the Brewers, then to the Royals. Jim had been forced to deal with the reality that batting success in the major leagues involves failing six or seven times out of every ten attempts. As he explained,

"I've worked through feeling like a failure. I've gained confidence through Christ, and I refuse to base my self-image on whether I get a certain number of hits. Instead, I base my worth on the fact that I'm loved by God. I was raised to think that baseball was everything; but in the past five or six years, I have begun to realize that other areas of life such as being a good husband and father are just as important."

Jim's statements reminded me of an interview I had with George Brett, who had flirted with the almost-impossible .400 batting average in 1980. Though he was having unparalleled success at the plate, George told me about his struggle to maintain confidence, since even at a .400 average he failed an average of six times out of every ten plate appearances. As believers we must maintain an attitude of confidence in Christ, even when life is difficult and failure frequent.

Second, we need to cultivate an attitude of contentment. That's the attitude Paul expressed in Philippians 4 when he conveyed his gratitude for the gift from the Philippian church. He explained that the important issue wasn't whether he had or didn't have certain things. What counted was his relationship with Christ, who had empowered him to handle any circumstance. That's why Paul had earlier pointed out to the Philippians the importance of always rejoicing no matter the circumstances (v. 4). What a practical antidote for the glum, sour feelings that often plague us at work today.

Third, positive attitudes can be reinforced with humor. The book of Proverbs explains how "a merry heart" provides incredible benefits, including a good countenance instead of a crushed spirit (15:13), a positive attitude that leads to successful actions instead of calamity (v. 15), and good health to counter the physical and emotional drought of a broken spirit (17:22). According to corporate consultant Leslie Gibson, the average four-year-old laughs four hundred times a day, whereas adults typically laugh only fifteen to sixteen times.[6] Just think of the speakers you enjoy or the colleagues you prefer to work with. Laughing with colleagues can often help us alleviate stress on the job.

For me, recording Back to the Bible's many overseas broadcasts can be stressful. But working with Herman Rohlfs, who possesses a keen wit, a great sense of humor, and a gracious spirit, has made that responsibility a delight. If the average adult laughs only fifteen to sixteen times a day, Herman and I usually surpass that mark during a single hour of overseas recording. Then we top things off by trading stories at coffee break, where we're usually joined by Allen Bean, chief researcher at Back to the Bible, who is always on the lookout for a clean, funny story. The three of us, plus our colleague Woodrow Kroll and our engineering team, have developed a humor-laced camaraderie that has sustained us through many a stressful recording session.

The Marriott Corporation has been recognized as one of the most successful companies in America. When he took over the corporate reins, Bill Marriott was given a number of guidelines by his father, company founder Jay Willard Marriott. These included the importance of thinking objectively and maintaining a sense of humor. As Jay succinctly put it, "Make the business fun for you and others."[7]

Unlike many business leaders of his era, Jay Marriott believed in the priority of people. As he advised his son, "People are number one—their growth, loyalty, and team spirit." He urged Bill to look for the good in people and try to develop those qualities, trust people, delegate, and hold them accountable for results.

This brings us to another practical suggestion: *We should always make people a higher priority than projects or process.* In other words, I need to think of people—myself and others—the way God thinks of them. Since God cared enough about me to pay the incredible price it took to secure my salvation, I need to recognize the value He has placed on me and other people. I'm to avoid becoming proud, but I need to discover and use the gifts God has given me.

Change and Growth

Someone has said that success and growth come from a series of small changes leading relentlessly toward the goals we have set. The right kind of realistic, positive attitude can be the key to such changes. Researchers at the University of California-Berkeley studied 142 men and women over a forty-year period. They found those who developed positive attitudes and active lifestyles when they were younger tended to remain active and happy as they aged. Those who were depressed, anxious, or had more negative attitudes were still struggling with the same problems forty years later.

If, as Solomon told us, we are as we think, and if we can change our thinking as Paul exhorted us to, then that's what we need to do—change our thinking. We need to see ourselves, our circumstances, and others the way God intends us to.

Practical Tips

Let me share some practical suggestions that can help you apply what we've been talking about to some of the stressful situations you face at work. First, begin to monitor your thought life. Whenever you start feeling negative, upset, or discouraged, don't just ignore the emotion. Look for the thoughts and beliefs behind it. Have you allowed a comment by your boss or a fellow worker to affect you? Or is it something totally outside the workplace?

Second, use negative thoughts as a signal to refocus. During the years when I worked with him on the radio, Dr. Frank Minirth must have repeated a simple axiom more than a hundred times. "Anxiety is a signal to relax and look for the source." To this day, whenever I feel myself growing anxious or uptight, I remember that axiom. Suppose you arrived at work this morning and a colleague gave you a piece of his mind he really couldn't afford to lose. Perhaps you had heard his story before—it didn't help you then and you found it even less helpful the second time. You could simply relax, refocus, and wait for an opportunity to respond appropriately.

Third, look for the explanation. Let's go back for a moment to that stressful dumping of thoughts and emotions by your colleague. Your natural conclusion might be, "I must be a terrible person. My fellow worker doesn't like me or what I am doing. I must be at fault."

When you find yourself thinking that way, it's important to consider other possible explanations. Maybe your colleague is having a battle with his chronic temper. Perhaps there is something he or she needs prayer about.

The fourth step is to reassess your values. Our thinking can become saturated with musts, shoulds, oughts, and have-tos. Some of these may be biblical and valid. Others we may have picked up from our parents or from circumstances—or even fabricated them ourselves. I recall how relieved I felt after a particularly difficult television taping session to hear my colleague Chris Thurman tell me, "I'm glad that happened. You survived a test in an area you find difficult, and you learned a few things in the process." I was feeling totally stressed out, overwhelmed by such thoughts as *I must be a terrible interviewer. I should have done better. I ought to be able to handle this in a more professional manner.* As we talked about our struggles with the oughts, shoulds, and musts of life, Chris explained the importance of cleaning up our thinking to include messages like, "I'm capable of doing better," "I would like to do better," and "Probably, next time I will do better. But my worth as a person isn't tied to how well I perform."

Finally, never give up. Some years ago I wrote a book by that title. Just after it appeared in print, the publisher was sold to a much larger corporation, which decided not to reprint the book. Soon after learning of the publisher's decision, I asked Al Zoller, director of publications for Back to the Bible, if the broadcast might like to publish it as a ministry tool.

Before long the decision had been made, the rights secured, and the book rushed back into print, complete with an attractive new cover. Imagine the surprise of those who had given up on *Never Give Up* when they learned that we had shipped fifteen thousand copies by the end of January 1995!

Of course, even in this principle we need to recognize a balancing factor. The book *Never Give Up* contains a chapter titled "When Hope Is Not Enough" which explains that there does come a time when we may need to give up on some things to move on to something else.

The key is to know when to quit, when to walk away, or when to keep fighting. Thirty-year-old Karen Ivory, a network television producer, loved the adrenaline high and the stress of working at WCBS Television in New York.[8] Sitting in the control room during live broadcasts, she found herself consumed with fear that a newscast would run too long or a live remote would go dead. Finally one winter day in 1986, she decided enough was enough—it was time to quit the stress of her high-pressure position. Taking charge of her life, she exchanged her network career for the more tranquil lifestyle of a public relations position at a small Pennsylvania college.

There is a time to keep going and a time to quit. With God's direction we can learn how to apply motivation and the right attitude to make the right decision.

The Control Factor

It seems we feel our stresses most keenly when we face the kind of circumstances and changes that leave us with a sense that things are out of control. But when you feel a sense of purpose and commitment in your life and work, and your attitude toward change is to view it as a challenge instead of seeing it as a threat, you are in a much better position to use stress to sharpen your endurance and your coping skills. In fact, a study of Fortune 500 CEOs showed their mortality rate was 37 percent lower than average, primarily be cause they felt in control and viewed change as a challenge.[9] The key, again, is attitude.

Just think about the difference between work and play. Ultimately it comes down to our attitude. After all, you use many of the same muscles to mow the lawn or play golf. You use the same brain power to play Monopoly® or conduct business. The difference comes down to mental attitude. Why does work tire us more easily than play? Mark Twain once said, "Work is not a concrete thing. It's a mental attitude. Nothing is either work or play, but thinking makes it so."[10]

General George Washington has been recognized as a master motivator. In 1777, his soldiers faced a cold, bleak winter of inactivity on a mountain near Morristown, New Jersey. Noting the signs of restlessness and grumbling among the troops, Washington told his engineering officers to quickly begin building a fort. Work on the fortifications started immediately, and the soldiers snapped out of their glum feelings and began speculating when the attack might come.

Finally the spring thaws began and General Washington ordered his men to prepare for a move, even though construction on the fort wasn't quite finished.

His chief of engineers asked, "General, will we move before the fort is finished?" Washington replied, "It has served its purpose. The fort was just nonsense to keep the men busy at something they thought important." The fort came to be known as "Fort Nonsense," even though it served an important purpose in maintaining the motivation and morale of Washington's troops.

According to Stephen Covey, the key to motivation is motive. It all comes down to the "why" that gives us the energy to stay strong in stressful moments. That's what provides the strength for us to say no when we need to as we connect with the motivation of a deeper yes burning inside.[11]

CHAPTER TWELVE

YOUR WORK AND PEOPLE

When we began our journey through stress in the workplace, we recognized several important stress-causing factors—changes, corporate downsizing, new technologies, and the demand to work more hours. Yet the most stressful thing about our work, at least from the perspective of most of the people with whom I have talked, involves relating to the people we work with. After all, each of our fellow workers is different from us. They all have different objectives, different needs. They view things differently, and that leads to stress.

Furthermore, just like us, they are all fallen. They have sin natures, capacities to engage in all kinds of sinful, conflict-producing behaviors, and harmful ways of relating.

FOCUS ON PEOPLE

Unfortunately, much of what has been written about personal achievement focuses on competition. We have been told how to "swim with the sharks" without being eaten and urged to cultivate leadership secrets from such dubious role models as Atilla the Hun. A modern distortion of the golden rule urges us to "Do unto others before they do unto you."

Our final chapter is designed to take us in a different direction, to focus on cooperation instead of competition, win-win in place of win-lose, and synergy and shared vision rather than autocratic handed-down vision. Earlier, we pointed out how many principles for dealing with stress in the workplace grow out of those fundamental mandates of loving God and loving our neighbors. In chapter 10 we looked at the importance of loving God with all our hearts and establishing values, priorities, and principles based on our love for Him. In the preceding chapter we discussed developing an appropriate way to think about ourselves, cultivating right attitudes and motivation. Now it's time to move beyond ourselves to "loving our neighbors" at work.

The Golden Rule

Early in His ministry, Jesus amplified this principle of relating to people in what we call the Golden Rule: "Therefore, whatever you want men to do to you, do also to them, for this is the Law and the Prophets" (Matthew 7:12).

Jesus is saying, "Treat people the way you want them to treat you." This principle was designed to summarize the essential teachings of the entire Old Testament. There's only one problem with this: Many of the people we live and work with are fallen, sinful people without the power of the indwelling Spirit or a commitment to live by the Word. The rest are believers who still struggle, experience persistent conflicts, and often fail to get a handle on relating to others.

Before we consider a structure for relating to people in the workplace, let's talk about a couple of strategies that don't work. One is forceful intimidation; the other is codependent manipulation.

Spend a few minutes browsing through the business or pop psychology section of your local bookstore, and you'll discover a wide range of books designed to teach you how to forcefully exert your will over other people. Read them, they promise, and you will learn to intimidate those around you, dominate conversations, and force your will on others.

While some may have identified elements of truth about assertiveness, most of their overall strategies are doomed to fail. The simple reason is that intimidation isn't the Lord's way. A person can learn how to intimidate and manipulate others, but such "victories" do not bring long-term benefit.

You may recall an occasion near the end of Jesus' ministry when James and John, urged on by their ambitious mother, cornered the Lord to demand places of special prominence in the coming kingdom. After all, they were prominent disciples and sons of Zebedee.

Jesus' response utterly destroyed the foundation of their appeal and established an alternative standard of excellence by which all human relations should be measured, then and now.

Jesus called them to Himself and said, "You know that the rulers of the Gentiles lord it over them, and those who are great exercise authority over them. Yet it shall not be so among you; but whoever desires to become great among you, let him be your servant. And whoever desires to be first among you, let him be your slave." (Matthew 20:25–27)

The Master's Mandate

Here was the Master's new mandate. His followers were to avoid the old way of prestige, power, and influence like the plague. Leadership according to the Master doesn't involve impressive titles or special perks but servant hearts and a willingness to reach out and care about others.

Some time ago I heard a story about an arrogant young Bible college student who insisted that the president of his college do something about the rest rooms in the men's dorm that were constantly stopped up. A short time lster, the young man was shocked to discover the president on his knees in the rest room, working on the plumbing. Here was a man who modeled a servant's heart.

A news reporter asked conductor Leonard Bernstein, "What is the most difficult instrument to play?" Bernstein replied without hesitation, "Second fiddle." Then he went on to explain: "I can easily get plenty of first violinists, but to find one who plays second violin with as much enthusiasm, or second French horn, or second flute—now that's a problem. But if no one plays second, we have no harmony."[1]

The Master clinched His argument with His men when He pointed out that even "the Son of Man did not come to be served, but to serve, and to give His life a ransom for many" (Matthew 20:28). Throughout His ministry, Jesus served people, allowing them to interrupt Him, reaching out in love to heal them, raising their dead, and freeing them from Satan's power. The night before His death He interrupted another discussion over who would be the greatest—He washed their feet the way the lowliest servant would have done. Then He served us all in the ultimate way, by dying on the cross to pay for our sins.

The appropriate way to greatness or influence isn't winning by intimidation. It's winning by servanthood.

DANGER: MANIPULATION

There is a far more subtle hazard we face as we relate to people at work and in life. It is the danger of becoming manipulative, of using rescuing, codependent strategies to get what we want out of others in inappropriate ways.

The term *codependency* grew out of studies of alcoholics and others who demonstrated clear patterns of addiction. It has been used primarily to describe those who haven't become addicted to alcohol or drugs but have demonstrated some kind of addiction or attraction to an addict and his or her bondage. One of the authors who helped coin the term, Melody Beattie, defines a codependent person as "one that has let another person's behavior affect him or her, and who is obsessed with controlling that person's behavior."[2]

 **STRESS TEST**

Your People Skills

Do you sometimes feel that your job would be great if you didn't have to deal with people (co-workers, clients, supervisors)? Or does your boss get upset at you for spending too much time talking and interacting with people? Maybe you fall somewhere in between: You enjoy interaction with other people, and you're good at it. To see whether you might have room for improvement, answer the following questions:

1. *Do you feel that your voice is heard at work?*

   YES   NO   SOMETIMES

2. *Do you treat others' insights with respect?*

   YES   NO   SOMETIMES

3. *Have you recently expressed approval of a co-worker's or subordinate's work?*   YES   NO   SOMETIMES

4. *Do your conversations with clients and outside professionals express that you care about more than their wallets or their skills?*   YES   NO   SOMETIMES

5. *Do you trust the people you work with? Can they trust you?*   YES   NO   SOMETIMES

6. *When someone else is talking with you, do you give him or her full attention, or do you tend to keep working with papers or the computer?*   YES   NO   SOMETIMES

7. *Do you return phone calls within a reasonable period of time?*   YES   NO   SOMETIMES

8. *Do you resolve conflict politely, quickly, and in a way where both parties feel respected?*   YES   NO   SOMETIMES

9. *Do you avoid gossip?*   YES   NO   SOMETIMES

10. *Are you willing to play "second fiddle" on a project? Do you give others who have worked with you appropriate credit or recognition?*   YES   NO   SOMETIMES

For the codependent, control is the primary issue. Since codependent people usually come from families with a fairly high level of dysfunction—all families are dysfunctional to some degree because of the Fall—they determine to use what works to win the acceptance and approval of others, especially the addict.

On the other hand, they feel driven to control the behavior of others, especially the addict. Experience has taught them that straightforward efforts to control others seldom work, so they use subtle techniques that range from guilt trips to lavish praise to sarcasm and even humor.

Most codependents have mastered a wide arsenal of tricks for controlling others. They may slip into the role of a nurturing codependent, lavishing attention and praise. At times they throw their weight around, barking orders, or they may use withdrawal to get their way. Basically, codependent individuals haven't learned where the healthy boundaries between themselves and other people should exist. As a result, their whole perspective on relationships is distorted—including relationships at work. Underlying codependent behavior is an incredible hunger for love, and an insatiable thirst for acceptance and worth. These feelings usually grow out of childhood pain or abuse and false beliefs that have distorted their view of life.

My purpose is not to rehash what has been written on this subject or attempt to plow new ground in an area some refer to as "pop psychology." Instead, I want to seek to apply an important biblical principal to a problem I believe lies at the heart of a great deal of conflict between people in the workplace. The principle is found in Galatians 6.

It can be difficult to distinguish healthy, loving help from codependent, manipulative entanglement. As we seek to serve God and people, we need to understand the difference between the servant who is committed to what is in the best interest of others and the person whose goal is to win the approval of others or get them to do what he or she wants.

The apostle Paul sheds significant light on this subject in Galatians 6 when he uses two phrases about bearing burdens. In verse 2 he explains how we are to "bear one another's burdens." Then in verse 5 he adds, "Each one shall bear his own load." In what seems to be a paradox, we discover the key to serving others without becoming manipulative or controlling. Before he discussed bearing each other's burdens, Paul called on spiritual believers to restore those who had been taken in some fault. The gist of his exhortation is that, when conflicts arise or failures occur, the problem should be addressed straightforwardly, not in a roundabout, manipulative manner. The goal is never to heap condemnation on an individual but to restore him to spiritual health. When others are overwhelmed and overloaded, we should be available to provide compassionate service (v. 2). On the other hand, everyone is expected to pull his share of the load, just like a soldier or hiker has a responsibility to carry his own pack (v. 5). This passage provides a biblical foundation for healthy interdependence that contrasts with both manipulative codependency and rugged independence.

What is the practical implication for our workplaces? I believe it is incumbent on us to reach a biblical balance. We need to beware of developing a "Rescue 911" mentality or a compulsion to care for everyone else to boost our own self-worth. We must also avoid developing the kind of individualism that refuses to help others.[3]

THE ENCOURAGER

Paul sent the church in Thessalonica a pair of letters containing strategic principles for dealing with relationships at work and in the church. In the first epistle he addressed the foundational issue of encouragement, pointing to his own life as an example of how encouragement was to work. Paul characterized his ministry as one of encouragement (1 Thessalonians 2:3) and further described it as pure of verbal deceit, uncleanness, or manipulation. As he described how the process of encouragement worked, Paul pointed out, "We were there with you along the way—called alongside to help you as part of God's family. Our goal was to avoid manipulative trickery, false motives, or throwing our weight around by intimidating you" (vv. 5–6, my paraphrase). Instead, the apostle explained, "In the gentle manner of a nursing mother, we shared our hearts with you" (vv. 7–8, my paraphrase).

In other words, Paul had practiced what Jesus preached about loving our neighbors as ourselves. Furthermore, he demonstrated his unconditional love for them by verbally encouraging them. As he explained in verse 11, "You know how we exhorted, and encouraged, and charged every one of you, as a father his children, that you would have a walk worthy of God who calls you into His own kingdom and glory." Later he urged them to "comfort each other and edify one another, just as you also are doing" (1 Thessalonians 5:11).

In essence, what Paul did was use his presence and his words to strengthen them. He was their encourager, called alongside to help. Perhaps you have heard about a tradition carried out by every Jewish soldier who completes basic training. These soldiers all complete a grueling fifty-mile hike to Masada, climb the massive peak, gather at the top, and end with a resounding cry, "Masada shall never fall again."

After hiking fifty miles through the desert, climbing Masada isn't easy, even for trained soldiers. But in the Israeli army, either everybody makes it or nobody does. The stronger members of each group carry, push, pull, and support the others so that even the weakest makes it to the top. In short, the men and women of the Israeli army have learned to practice true encouragement—to be called alongside to help.

So how does this process impact stress in the workplace? Encouragement provides a foundation for resolving conflict. When people are out of line, they need to be admonished or lovingly confronted. When those around us are about to give up, they need to be cheered up and encouraged to keep on, just as Paul encouraged his comrades on the ship in Acts 27 not to give up. Furthermore, those with particular weaknesses need to be helped in their struggle to deal with those weaknesses. Every human being, in every relationship, will require patience. That's why Paul concluded with the reminder, "Be patient toward all" (1 Thessalonians 5:14).

Think what a difference it would make if we applied these principles to resolve conflicts and problems at work. When people get out of line, instead of gossiping about them we would go directly to them in love—first individually, then, if necessary, with a witness to lovingly confront them with the goal of restoring, rather than destroying, them.

Imagine the impact when we share words of cheer and affirmation with fellow employees who are going through difficult times and feel like giving up. Consider the positive result of providing help and support to those at our workplaces who have long-term weaknesses.

Verbal Encouragement

We cannot consider the subject of encouragement without recognizing that much of what we are talking about is verbal—the use of kind, supportive words to build others up. Remember what the author of Proverbs said about the impact of our words on others: "Death and life are in the power of the tongue" (18:21). In fact, words have the power to either kill or heal. "There is one who speaks like the piercings of a sword, but the tongue of the wise promotes health" (12:18). In the New Testament Paul urged believers to "speak the truth in love" (Ephesians 4:15).

Two other essential skills for verbal support are listening and conflict resolution. Long ago I remember hearing someone say that God gave us two ears and one mouth so we could learn to listen more than we spoke. Since I'm a fairly verbal person, I've had to work on this. Perhaps you have as well. I've found it helpful to review the warning that we need to be quick to hear, slow to speak, and slow to anger (James 1:19). Paul urged the Thessalonians to "aspire to lead a quiet life" (1 Thessalonians 4:11), and Solomon pointed out that "a soft answer turns away wrath, but a harsh word stirs up anger" (Proverbs 15:1).

It has been said that we listen at between four and six times the rate most people speak. It's easy to become distracted while others speak and begin to think of other things, or even start planning what to say in response. We must work at paying complete attention, listening not only to what is being said, but looking for underlying messages that may be communicated by body language or tone of voice.

This also means resisting the temptation to chime in before the person we're listening to is finished. As Solomon said, "He who answers a matter before he hears it, it is folly and shame to him" (Proverbs 18:13).

When it comes to those we work with, it is important to listen with prudence and discretion. Practice keeping confidences. Also, be careful to evaluate the appropriateness of any personal confidences shared in a working environment. Sometimes things are best discussed off the job, or it may be wiser to refer the person who seeks to talk over a problem with us to a pastor or Christian counselor for additional help.

How should we deal with those inevitable disagreements that come up on the job? In Ephesians 4 Paul presents a series of principles for conflict resolution that hold many implications for the workplace as well as home and the church.

First, always practice honesty and mutual respect. "Therefore, putting away lying, each one speak truth with his neighbor, for we are members of one another" (Ephesians 4:25). Paul had already established the importance of speaking the truth in love (v. 15). Now he provides the rationale behind this balanced approach to communication. Since we are members of one another in the body of Christ, we should communicate honestly and respectfully.

"But wait," you may counter. "The people with whom I find myself in conflict at work are not believers." That may be true, but you and they are members of the same work team.

Furthermore, the principle of speaking the truth in love seems to have been Paul's recommended style of communicating with believer and nonbeliever alike. Thus, honesty and mutual respect are to provide the foundation for communicating with our boss, our fellow workers, and with others.

Second, don't use prolonged or deadly force. "'Be angry, and do not sin': do not let the sun go down on your wrath" (Ephesians 4:26). According to the following verse, when we do so we allow Satan to get a foothold—and what a deadly thing to have happen in a working environment. Some practical implications include not "gunny-sacking" conflicts or grievances—storing them up so we can use them later to fuel vengeance or efforts to get even. Nor should we pretend that no problem exists. Other deadly communications strategies to avoid include practicing prolonged "freeze outs," attacking or belittling, rejecting another person without attempting to correct the problem, exaggerating an issue, denying the emotions we feel in a conflict, or allowing a conflict to persist without trying to deal with it.

Third, let negative problems lead to positive solutions. "Let no corrupt communication proceed out of your mouth, but what is good for necessary edification, that it may impart grace to the hearers" (Ephesians 4:29). Paul calls for an evaluation of the quality and integrity of our verbal communication in the same way my wife evaluates fresh vegetables at the supermarket or the farmers' market. She is always careful that they don't just look good on the outside but are not corrupt or spoiled inside. Ask yourself, *Is what I am saying really good? Does it have lasting value? Does it measure up to God's character?* A second criteria is, Does it edify? Will it build up others, or does it tear them down? If my communication has taken a corrupt or negative direction, can I turn it around to make it edifying? Third, will it give grace or enablement to those who hear it? Will it serve as a positive reinforcement, or are my words themselves corrupt? This warning parallels Paul's cautions in Ephesians 5:4 about appropriate use of language—"neither filthiness, nor foolish talking, nor coarse jesting, which are not fitting, but rather giving of thanks." What an important element to help us maintain a good testimony in our relationships with others at work.

Fourth, beware of destructive verbal blasts that grieve the Spirit and devastate others. We can wreak incredible harm with just a few well-chosen, sarcastically barbed, poison-tipped words. That's why Paul warns against bitterness, rage, clamoring, anger, slander, and ill will. It is easy to explode in anger when subordinates fail to meet a deadline, get into shouting matches when others present views that counter our objectives, engage in slandering, or allow bitterness or ill will to develop toward fellow workers. Instead, I need to house-clean my attitudes and my verbal actions so that I can avoid grieving God's Spirit and harming those around me.

Fifth, walk in forgiving love. The apostle calls for three cardinal virtues: kindness, or what is suitable for meeting others' needs; compassion, or tender inner emotions rather than a callused "hard-edged" approach to people; and forgiveness—the same gracious action God extended to us based on the sacrificial death of His Son.

Shared Vision

But can we move beyond just resolving our inevitable conflicts to develop authentic interdependence and mutual support? Is there some concept that can take us beyond the interpersonal stresses of our workplace to get us working together in a way that the whole is greater than the sum of the parts? There is, and we might label it "shared vision."

We live much of our lives interdependently with other people—spouses, parents, children, friends, bosses, employees, co-workers, neighbors, fellow church members. And as we have already noted, the Bible places a premium on relationships and interdependence. Unfortunately, many Christians have developed a "lone ranger" approach to Christianity. Instead of depending on others in the body of Christ, they somehow have come to feel that God values rugged individualism. At times we take this mentality into our workplace.

Underlying biblical interdependence is the important concept called "trust." In interpersonal relationships, trust requires a high degree of loyalty, honesty, commitment, and integrity. Stephen Covey tells how he learned a lesson in trust and loyalty from the president of a university in Hawaii. When he arrived to give an extended lecture series, he found the housing situation not what he expected. His response: "I went in and complained to the president about his housing director. I was critical and upset."[4]

According to Covey, the man listened with respect, then said, "Stephen, I'm so sorry to hear about this, but my housing director is such a fine, competent person. Let's have him come over here, and we will solve this together." As Covey explained it, he wasn't interested in meeting with the housing director. He just wanted to complain, and he wanted the president to fix the situation. But by the time the housing director had arrived, and they had met and resolved the situation, he felt subdued, humbled, and somewhat embarrassed.

"Oh, what respect I felt for that president, who sustained his people, spoke positively about them, and wanted them involved in the process of resolving any negative issues. That president was principle-centered. I knew that if someone were ever to complain about me in his presence—in any capacity—he would treat me with the same respect. This man was loyal to those who were absent." Furthermore, the president had not only trusted his director, he had cultivated a relationship in which he and the other directors could share directly in his goals and solutions.

Loyalty and trust are foundational to shared vision. Trust and trustworthiness are essential if we are to move beyond mere peaceful coexistence at work to the point where shared vision takes root and bears fruit.

In *First Things First,* Covey uses a tree to illustrate how individuals can work interdependently to fulfill their specific roles. The roots represent foundational principles, the trunk is the mission, and the branches are the specific roles.[5] As Covey points out, "Nature teaches of a larger interdependent balance. The tree itself is part of a huge ecosystem. Its well-being affects and is affected by the well-being of other living things around it. The reality of this interdependence makes it vital to recognize each role as a stewardship."[6]

Covey's analogy from nature parallels Paul's description of interdependence in the body of Christ in Ephesians 4 and 1 Corinthians 12. Paul's point is that our place in the body of Christ and our connection with God (Ephesians 4:4–6), plus our individual giftedness and unique abilities (vv. 7–11), have been designed to enable us to serve others and build up the body of Christ (v. 12). God's ultimate aim is to produce interpersonal unity, personal spiritual growth, doctrinal and character stability, and Christlike maturity in a setting in which every believer has something to contribute (vv. 12–16). Maybe you thought that synergy and shared vision were concepts invented by modern-day leadership gurus. Not only did God originate these concepts, but He also had Paul write them down to guide our relationships in the body of Christ and provide us with a foundation for serving God on the job (see Ephesians 6:5–9).

In *The Seven Habits of Highly Effective People* and *First Things First*, Stephen Covey presents a simple, three-step principle-based process designed to lead to shared vision. First, think win-win. Second, seek first to understand, then to be understood. Third, synergize based on valuing differences and searching for third alternatives. Covey relates win-win to the Golden Rule and much of what is respected as wisdom literature. As he puts it, "As we learn to think win-win, we seek for mutual benefit in all our interactions. We start thinking in terms of other people, of society as a whole. It profoundly affects what we see as 'important,' how we spend our time, . . . and the results we get in our lives."[7]

In response we should ask, Are these concepts biblical? When we relate them to the foundational principle of loving your neighbor as yourself, they are, especially if we understand the definition of love. The essence of love involves a choice, a decision to seek the highest good for others. If I love my neighbor as myself, I will value or cherish that person and seek to meet his needs, or nourish him. Paul presents this as the way husbands should relate to their wives (Ephesians 5:25–29). It seems to me that the way he applies them in the marriage relationship, moving from the general principle of "submitting to one another in the fear of God" (v. 21) to specifics, gives us a ground for applying these principles to relationships with others, including at work.

Part of win-win involves an attitude of mutual submission and supportive love. Authentic Christian love seeks to develop Christlikeness in others—by sharing our faith with those who do not know the Savior or by seeking to build and strengthen maturity in those who do. It involves treating people with value and seeking to meet their needs. When we take this approach, the result isn't "I win, you lose," or "You win, I lose." The end result is synergy, or win-win. It leads to the kind of team building Joe Batten talks about as "primary among the qualities that lift great leaders above second-raters and also-rans." Batten calls for the building of work teams with transcendent focus, unity, loyalty, shared-strengths emphasis, and a high level of committed energy.[8]

Covey's second win-win principle, seek first to understand, then to be understood, also has roots in biblical concepts—valuing others, listening to them, and developing an understanding of them. As the old Indian proverb says, we shouldn't criticize another until we have walked a mile in his moccasins. As we listen, we not only gain understanding, we create an environment in which we can be understood. And when both people understand both perspectives, instead of being on opposite sides, we find ourselves on the same side looking at solutions together. As Covey puts it, "Real listening shows respect. It creates trust."[9]

When win-win thinking and seeking first to understand are in place, the result is a synergy that is more powerful than energy. Covey describes it as "the combined power of synergistic creative imagination, the almost magical math where one plus one equals three or more. . . . It is the creation of third alternatives that are genuinely better than solutions individuals could ever come up with on their own."[10]

A classic biblical example of this kind of shared vision can be seen in the ministry of Barnabas and Paul. In the church at Antioch, a large number of believers had come to the Lord, and there was much work to be done to encourage and strengthen those individuals. So the church leaders in Jerusalem sent Barnabas to Antioch, where he worked as hard as possible to help as many as he could (Acts 11:22–24).

However, it didn't take long for Barnabas to realize that the job was bigger than he could handle alone. So he took time off to travel to Tarsus to seek out Saul. He brought him to Antioch, and over an entire year the two men worked together, sharing a vision to encourage and equip believers (Acts 11:25–30). The product of that shared vision was far greater than what either individual could have accomplished alone. And Luke notes the ultimate result: the disciples were first called Christians in Antioch. So the label we hang on believers today resulted from the synergistic shared vision of a Levite from Cyprus and a Benjamite from Tarsus.

MENTORING AND EMPOWERMENT

This passage also contains another solution to the people aspect of stress—mentoring. Much has been written on the subject in our day, and it is not the purpose of this book to deal in-depth with mentoring. However, when we consider the amount of time Jesus invested in His disciples and examine the specific elements He built into His relationship with them—elements he expanded in John 17 in His final prayer before His arrest, trial, and crucifixion—it is clear that the Lord in effect "wrote the book" on how to mentor.[11]

Another key concept, closely related, is empowerment. Empowerment is the logical outgrowth of trust in the workplace, the kind that is cultivated as we demonstrate character —integrity, maturity, and competence. Competence is the knowledge and skill to achieve results, work through problems together, and discover new alternatives. Covey identifies several conditions necessary for empowerment to take place in a company or organization. They include trust and trustworthiness and win-win "stewardship agreements" that spell out the expected results, guidelines, resources, accountability, and consequences of success or failure.[12]

The classic biblical empowerment took place when Jesus charged His followers with the responsibility to witness about Him from Jerusalem to the ends of the earth—then provided them with the power and authority they needed to succeed in the person of the indwelling Spirit (Acts 1:5). It was an authentic stewardship agreement. They were to function as a team, each empowered to fulfill his own part, each responsible to the leaders—the apostles—and ultimately to the Master Himself. And the synergy—the combined result— would surpass the capabilities of any of them as individuals, even though each had an individual stake, including promised rewards, in successfully fulfilling the Master's mandate.

The Lord's mission for the church provides a remarkable illustration of how empowerment and shared vision can function in workplaces today. Accountability must be in place, structures and systems aligned, and a team concept at work. Every team member must be a stakeholder—one who shares the company's vision and objectives, who feels like and is a significant player in producing a successful outcome.

Implementing this kind of team concept can be difficult in organizations where things have operated in a more hierarchical fashion for a long time. But it is a concept that can work. Paul and Barnabas used it to carry out the most successful missionary movement ever.

Recently we began using the team concept at Back to the Bible to implement a number of changes in an organization that for more than fifty-six years has been fulfilling its mission of touching the world by teaching the Word. When the decision was made to implement several strategic changes, everyone up and down the management line, including Woodrow Kroll, the CEO, and the directors, bought into the transition. I was brought on board to serve in a newly established role— cohost and producer of the daily broadcast. I was given a position that didn't fit the traditional management line. Although I would answer to the director of broadcasting, my role as program producer was designed to give me the freedom to operate "outside the lines," working directly with nonmanagement engineering and production personnel, management and director-level supervisors, and the general director and Bible teacher himself. With my responsibility focused on the program, I was given the mandate to put together a production team that would ensure quality in the changes we were making and promised regular feedback. I was given the trust to fulfill this mandate and get the job done.

In turn, I entrusted different aspects of our production to members of the broadcast team, people who felt themselves a valuable part of the change process and the production. My team was given the resources and freedom to implement changes that everyone "bought into." Those changes included reducing the music content and adding missions features and supplementary interviews gradually rather than all at once, which made our task somewhat more difficult. Because we were able to function as a team, meet as a team, support each other, and hold each other accountable, we were able to successfully bring about these substantive changes. We maintained Back to the Bible's historic role of "teaching the Word and touching the world" while improving the way we support the Bible teaching and communicate the vision for impacting the world with the message of Christ.

For me it has been one of the most exciting aspects of my years in ministry, seeing problems resolved, people working and praying together, sharing a vision for this ministry. However, I can hear some of you saying, "But, Don, you're talking about a Christian organization, a place where you expect things to work out 'happily ever after.'"

Two responses come to mind. First, Christian workplaces aren't necessarily ideal, or even any more free of problems than the average secular workplace. Second, the same principles we've been talking about can be used in either kind of work environment. After all, I'm convinced that loving our neighbor as ourselves—the bedrock foundational principle on which this entire chapter is based—relates to believer and unbeliever alike.

UNIVERSAL NEED

Everyone needs encouragement and support. Everybody feels the pressure of life, the hardships of living in a fallen world. Everyone needs to be motivated toward moral and spiritual excellence. The more we encourage each other, set examples, and lovingly share God's principles for living, the better we are able to affect those around us—whether they need to trust Christ as Savior or live for Him as Lord.

Furthermore, all of us need resources and help for personal growth and problem solving. We all face difficulties on the job. It's the nature of the beast. There will be times when we struggle with our work—especially since other people are involved. If we provide an environment in which individuals can strengthen each other, accept each other, and motivate each other, the result can be a workplace in which we not only find stress relieved but positive changes taking place, with solutions that go far beyond anything we could imagine.

Let me provide a final example, a situation in which you

may be able to apply some of the principles we have talked about in this chapter.

Suppose for months you have had concerns about a member of your staff. His work seems to be slipping, and at times his attitude hasn't been what it could. You've been praying for an opportunity to talk to him while attempting to model concern, but not pushing things.

One afternoon shortly after lunch this employee brings in a report and places it on your desk. In the casual interchange that follows, he begins to open up and share deeply about the pain and frustration that has been affecting his work. You are delighted but quickly began to feel uncomfortable because in a few minutes you are scheduled to begin an important meeting with your boss and his boss.

Situations like this typically cause a great deal of frustration and anxiety. We feel caught in a dilemma, pulled in different directions. Suppose you decide to take the time to listen to your employee and come to the meeting late. But your boss's boss has a reputation for being upset with people who are late for meetings. So you might be tempted to look at your watch and say, "I'm really sorry. I have to rush off to a meeting"—perhaps even send the employee off rather abruptly to Human Resources with his problem.

But what about the loyalty and value of that employee? The motivation and creativity of this individual could be stifled. How will he feel about you as a person of worth, and especially as a person who values him? You are faced with a moment of choice. What do you do?

You know God wants you to please your boss. That's biblical. You also know that loving your neighbor as yourself, caring enough to be interruptible, and taking time for an individual are also biblical.

So you ask yourself, *What's the most important thing to do right now?* As you do, you ask God for wisdom. In a situation like this, it's hard to be sure what's most important. People are more important than schedules. But there are also people involved in the scheduled meeting—including your boss's boss.

You ask, "How does this affect my circle of influence?" The answer is, both fit your circle of influence. Both are related to your personal and vocational mission and purposes.

Next you ask yourself, *What principles apply?* The principles that come to mind are be honest and open, involve the people the problem affects, and work out solutions together rather than arbitrarily handing down a solution.

As you ask God for wisdom, you may say to the employee, calling him by name, "I appreciate your willingness to share these deep concerns. This is so important, I want to have time to talk it over with you and work with you to find solutions. But I have another concern, because I've made a commitment to some other people to meet with them right now. My meeting should be over by 3:00, though. How would you feel about getting together at that time to talk this through?"

As an alternative, you might ask your employee to wait a moment while you ask your secretary or associate to walk to the meeting and explain that something important has come up and you need to be a half hour late. You could even request that your agenda items be shifted to the end of the meeting—or you may call in an associate and ask him or her to represent you at the meeting.

Or perhaps as you pause, you realize that the concerns of this employee aren't in your direct area of responsibility. So you may feel the best thing to do is to walk with the employee over to Human Resources where those needs or concerns can be better addressed.

The important thing is that what you have done is ask God for wisdom, which is what James 1:5 is all about. Since James was writing to encourage believers under stress, I believe there is a direct correlation between handling the stressful situations that come up at work—including those involving people—and seeking wisdom. Most important, when we ask God for wisdom, He promises to give it to us, and that includes the wisdom to deal effectively with stress in our workplace.

NOTES

Chapter 1: Stressed-Out and Overworked

1. Andrea Stone and Tom Squitieri, "Bomb Forces Question: How Safe Are We?" *USA Today*, 21 April 1995, 1–2A.
2. The first two books were coauthored with Frank Minirth and Paul Meier and published by Moody Press. The most recent (1992), *The Stress Factor*, was coauthored with Minirth and Meier and published by Northfield Press.
3. Hans Selye, *The Stress of Life*, rev. ed. (New York: McGraw-Hill, 1976), 74.
4. Julia Lawlor, "Workers Want to Get a Life," *USA Today*, 3 September 1993, 1–2B.
5. Ibid., 1B–2B.
6. Ibid.
7. Diane Kinde, "Workers Stressed Out, National Survey Finds," *Dallas Morning News*, 3 September 1993, 1A.
8. Lee Smith, "Burned Out Bosses," *Fortune*, 25 July 1994, 44–46.
9. Ibid.
10. Ibid.
11. Patty Beutler, "Some Folks Thrive on Stress While Others Are Undone by It," *Lincoln Journal Star*, 17 February 1995, 11X.

12. See Archibald D. Hart, *The Crazy Making Workplace* (Ann Arbor, Mich.: Servant, 1993), 139–140. Another study by Hart of the effects of stress is *The Hidden Link Between Adrenaline and Stress* (Dallas: Word, 1991).

13. Hart, *The Crazy Making Workplace*, 143.

14. We can also have renewed thinking that combats stress by recalling and accepting the apostle Paul's confidence in 2 Timothy 1:12 that the one whom we have believed "is able to keep what [we] have committed to Him until that Day."

Chapter 2: It's a Rat Race Out There

1. Richard Friedman and James McCaughran, "Psychogenic Hypertension," *Stress Medicine* 1 (January–March 1985): 5–8.

2. J. H. Merle D'Aubigne, *The Life and Times of Martin Luther* (Chicago: Moody, 1978), 11–13.

3. Annetta Miller, "Stress on the Job," *Newsweek*, 25 April 1988, 40.

4. Jeffrey Weiss, "Myriad Woes Put Dallas Under Pressure," *Dallas Morning News*, 24 February 1991, sec. J.

5. Ibid.

6. Albert B. Crenshaw, "The Myth of the Mobile Workforce," *Washington Post* 28 December 1994.

7. Anastasia Toufexis, "When People Fight Firing with Fire," *Time*, 25 April 1994, 35.

8. Juliet Schor, *The Overworked American* (New York: HarperCollins, 1992), 29.

9. Randolf Heaster, "Working Overtime or Overworking?" *Kansas City Star*, 15 November 1994, A12

10. Aaron Benstein and Wendy Zellner, *Business Week*, 17 July 1995, 55.

11. Ibid., 57.

12. Bruce Steinberg as quoted in "Did You Know That . . . " *Board Room Reports*, 1 April 1995, 15.

13. "Rate Your Stress Life," *Redbook* (June 1990): 83–89.

14. *The World Almanac and Book of Facts* (Mahwah, New Jersey: Funk & Wagnalls, 1994), 71b. The dollar amount to raise a child is based on projected annual expenditures and current dollars on a child born in 1990 to a married couple.

15. Jim Conway, *Men in Mid-life Crisis* (Elgin, Ill.: Cook, 1978), 29–30.
16. Gail Sheehy, *Passages* (New York: Duttand, 1974), 30–31.
17. "Dear Abby," *Lincoln Journal Star*, 22 April 1995, Sec. B6. Used by permission.
18 "Rate Your Stress Life," *Redbook*, 85.
19. Walter DeSmet, "Stress and the Missionary," *The Gospel Message* 1 (1988): 2.
20. Jim Lowry, "Survey Shows 2,100 Pastors Fired During Past 18 Months," *Baptist Standard*, 30 November 1988, 5.

Chapter 3: What Stress Does to Us

1. Sue Shellenbarger, "Work and Family," *Wall Street Journal*, 1 February 1995, B1.
2. Archibald Cox, "Are You Addicted to Adrenaline?" *Contact* 46 (December 1987/January 1988): 15.
3. Elizabeth Stark, "Stress," *American Health* (December 1992): 48.
4. "SmithKline Bid for Drugs Clears 2 FDA Panels," *Wall Street Journal*, 28 March 1995, A3.
5. Lisa Schroepper, "Below-the-Belt Stress," *American Health* (October 1990): 47.
6. Sue Brandon, "Is Your Job Making You Sick?" *Woman's Day*, 27 June 1995, 72.
7. Ibid.
8. Bruce Neuharth, "Stressed for Success," *Contact* 46 (December 1987/January 1988): 11.
9. Ibid., 13.
10. David M. Cooney, "Stress: It's Up to You," *Vital Speeches of the Day*, 12 November 1993, 238.
11. "Newspoints," *Black Enterprise* (February 1994): 34.
12. Bernard Baumohl, "Workers Who Fight Fire with Fire," *Time*, 25 April 1994, 36.
13. See Anastasia Toufexis, "When People Fight Firing with Fire," *Time*, 25 April 1994, 36.
14. "Work: It's a Killer," *Black Enterprise* (February 1994): 74.
15. Richard Blow, "Stamped Out," *New Republic*, 10 & 17 January 1994, 11.

16. "Loner in 30's Called Typical Workplace Killer," *New York Times*, 19 December 1993, 1:27

17. "Four Fatally Wounded in Holdup at Post Office," *Lincoln Journal Star*, 22 March 1995, 2A.

18. See Toufexis, "When People Fight Firing with Fire," 35–36.

19. "Man Shoots Wife, Kills Rival, Self," *Lincoln Journal Star*, 8 January 1995, 10A.

20. "Violence: America's Plague," *Society* (January–February 1994): 3.

21. Miriam Pepper, "Heartland Questions Safety in Work Place," *Time*, 25 April 1994, 36.

22. Sylvia Gearing, *Female Executive Stress Syndrome* (Fort Worth, Tex.: The Summit Group, 1995).

23. Bryan Knowles, "Job Versus Family: Striking a Balance," *Focus on the Family*, 19 June 1991, 2–4.

24. Ibid.

25. "The Best Stressed List," *Psychology Today* 25 (November/December 1992): 10.

26. Mortimer R. Feinberg, "Career Versus Family," *Board Room Reports*, 1 April 1995, 13.

Chapter 4: Back to Eden: Where Stress Began

1. John F. Walvoord and Roy B. Zuck, eds., *Bible Knowledge Commentary* (Wheaton, Ill.: Victor, 1985), 28.

2. Ibid., 30.

3. As quoted in Elisabeth Elliot, *Passion and Purity* (Old Tappan, N.J.: Revell, 1984).

Chapter 5: Back to the Fall: Where Bad Stress Began

1. Hans Selye, *The Stress of Life*, rev. ed. (New York: McGraw-Hill, 1956), 3.

2. Ibid., 55, 63.

3. Ibid., 63.

4. Ibid., 37.

5. Eric Allen, "Stress," *Contact* 46 (December 1987/January 1988): 3, 74.

6. "Looking at the Roots," *Time*, 25 May 1993, 23.

7. Stephen Covey, A. Roger Merrill, and Rebecca R. Merrill, *First Things First: A Principle-Centered Approach to Time & Life Management* (New York: Simon & Schuster, 1994), 169.
8. Victor Frankl, *Man's Search for Meaning* (New York: Pocket, 1959), 104.

Chapter 6: Pressures and Perceptions

1. Robert McGee, *The Search for Significance* (Waco, Tex.: Word, 1990).
2. "Stress," *Men's Health* 8 (November 1993): 63.
3. Ibid.
4. "Mind & Body," *Prevention* (April 1994): 41.

Chapter 7: Priorities and Urgencies

1. Stephen R. Covey, A. Roger Merrill, and Rebecca R. Merrill, *First Things First: A Principle-Centered Approach to Time & Life Management* (New York: Simon & Schuster, 1994), 88–89.
2. Ibid., 32.
3. Zig Ziglar, *Over the Top* (Nashville: Oliver Nelson, 1994), 181.
4. Ibid., 182.
5. Covey et al., *First Things First*, 37.
6. Ibid., 51–54.
7. Ibid., 170.
8. Thomas J. Peters and Robert H. Waterman, Jr., *In Search of Excellence* (New York: Warner, 1982), 14–16.
9. "Work, Work, Work: Long Hours May Stem from Too Many Distractions," *The Lincoln Star,* 17 January 1995, 5.

Chapter 8: Personalities (Yours and Others)

1. Florence Littauer and Marita Littauer, *Personality Puzzle* (Grand Rapids: Revell, 1992), 23.
2. Tim LaHaye, *The Spirit Controlled Temperament* (Wheaton, Ill.: Tyndale, 1966).
3. Frank B. Minirth and Paul D. Meier, *An Introduction to Psychology and Counseling* (Grand Rapids: Baker, 1982), 201–29.
4. Mark A. Pearson, *Why Can't I Be Me?* (Grand Rapids: Chosen Books, 1992), 29–46.

5. Ken Voges and Ron Braund, *Understanding How Others Misunderstand You* (Chicago: Moody, 1990), 38–42.

6. Gary Smalley and John Trent, *The Two Sides of Love* (Colorado Springs: Focus on the Family, 1992).

7. Voges and Braund, *Understanding How Others Misunderstand You*, 112.

8. "The Boss From Hell," *Working Woman*, December 1991.

9. Littauer and Littauer, *Personality Puzzle*, 116–17.

10. Frank Minirth, Paul Meier, Don Hawkins, Chris Thurman, and Richard Flournoy, *The Stress Factor* (Chicago: Northfield, 1992), 56ff.

Chapter 9: The Peter Principle and Stress

1. Laurence J. Peter and Raymond Hall, *The Peter Principle* (New York: William Morrow, 1969), 20.

2. Ibid., 25.

3. Ibid., viii.

4. *The Oxford American Dictionary* (New York, Avon Books: 1980), 411.

5. Laurence J. Peter, *The Peter Prescription* (New York: William Morrow, 1972), 92.

6. Ibid., 93.

7. Ibid., 44.

8. W. E. Vine, *A Depository Dictionary of Biblical Words* (Nashville: Nelson, 1984), 128.

9. Peter, *The Peter Prescription*, 57.

Chapter 10: Your Work and God

1. Marilyn vos Savant, "Ask Marilyn," *Parade*, 18 September 1994, 8.

2. Ibid.

3. Jon Johnston, *Christian Excellence* (Grand Rapids: Baker, 1985), 38.

4. R. W. Livingstone, *Greek Ideals in Modern Life* (London: Oxford Univ., n.d.), 88.

5. Johnston, *Christian Excellence*, 48.

6. Jerry Bridges, *The Pursuit of Holiness*, as quoted in Jon Johnston, *Christian Excellence* (Grand Rapids: Baker, 1985), 66.

7. Robert L. Young, *Analytical Concordance to the Bible* (Grand Rapids: Eerdmans, 1969), 351–53.

8. Doug Sherman and William Hendricks, *Your Work Matters to God* (Colorado Springs: Navpress, 1987), 205–6.

9. Ibid., 206.

10. Francis Brown, S. R. Driver, and C. A. Briggs, *A Hebrew and English Lexicon of the Old Testament* (Oxford: Clarion Press, 1907), 134–35, 180.

11. James Strong, *A Concise Dictionary of Words in the Hebrew Bible*, companion to *Strong's New Exhaustive Concordance of the Bible* (Nashville: Nelson, 1984).

12. Bruce Neuharth, "Stressed for Success," *Contact* 46 (December 1987/January 1988), 13.

13. Stephen Covey, A. Roger Merrill, and Rebecca R. Merrill, *First Things First: A Principle-Centered Approach to Time & Life Management* (New York: Simon & Schuster, 1994), 112.

14. William W. Biggs, "Spiritual Solutions for Stress," *Contact* 46 (December 1987/January 1988), 18.

15. Ibid., 19.

Chapter 11: Attitudes and Motivation

1. Zig Ziglar, *Over the Top* (Nashville: Oliver Nelson, 1994), 114–16.

2. Ibid., 115.

3. Robert L. Young, *Analytical Concordance to the Bible* (Grand Rapids: Eerdmans, 1969), 977.

4. Ted W. Engstrom, *Your Gift of Administration* (Nashville: Nelson, 1983), 87–88.

5. Ibid., 92–93.

6. Ziglar, *Over the Top*, 128.

7. Quoted in Joe Batten, *Tough-Minded Leadership* (New York: American Management Association, 1989), 12–13.

8. Annetta Miller, "Stress on the Job," *Newsweek*, 25 April 1988, 45.

9. Kathy Koontz, "Beating Burnout," *Success* (May 1986): 31.

10. Paul Lee Tan, *Encyclopedia of 7700 Illustrations* (Rockville, Md.: Assurance, 1979), 864.

11. Stephen Covey, A. Roger Merrill, and Rebecca R. Merrill, *First Things First: A Principle-Centered Approach to Time & Life Management* (New York: Simon & Schuster, 1994), 142.

Chapter 12: Your Work and People

1. Charles Swindoll, *Improving Your Serve* (Waco, Tex.: Word, 1981), 34.
2. Melody Beattie, *Codependent No More* (New York: Hazelden, 1987), 31.
3. For a more detailed discussion of these concepts, see chapter 11 in my book *Friends in Deed* (Chicago: Moody, 1994).
4. Stephen Covey also tells this story in Stephen Covey, A. Roger Merrill, and Rebecca R. Merrill, *First Things First: A Principle-Centered Approach to Time & Life Management* (New York: Simon & Schuster, 1994), 204.
5. Ibid., 224.
6. Ibid., 125.
7. Ibid., 129.
8. Joe Batten, *Tough-Minded Leadership* (New York: American Management Association, 1989), 106.
9. Covey et al., *First Things First,* 214.
10. Ibid., 215.
11. For a complete discussion of Jesus' mentoring concepts with His men, see my book *Master Discipleship* (Grand Rapids: Kregel, 1995).
12. Covey et al., *First Things First,* 224.

Moody Press, a ministry of the Moody Bible Institute, is designed for education, evangelization, and edification. If we may assist you in knowing more about Christ and the Christian life, please write us without obligation: Moody Press, c/o MLM, Chicago, Illinois 60610.